# The Boy From Brazil

### The Return of a Prodigal Son

## Marcelo Sousa

Dickens House Publishing

Copyright © 2022 by Dickens House Publishing

www.theboyfrombrazil.org

ISBN: 978-0-578-95505-6 (Paperback)

Library of Congress Control Number: 2022915597

First Edition

Illustrated by Steven Brahma

All Rights Reserved. No part of this publication may be reproduced, distributed, or transmitted in any form or by any means, including photocopying, recording, or other electronic or mechanical methods, without the prior written permission of the publisher, except in the case of brief quotations embodied in critical reviews and certain other noncommercial uses permitted by copyright law.

This book is protected under the copyright laws of the United States and other countries. Unauthorized reproduction or distribution of this book, or any portion of it, may result in severe civil and criminal penalties

For information on bulk purchases or speaking events, please contact:

Marcelo Sousa

Email: info@theboyfrombrazil.org

# Contents

| | |
|---|---|
| Special Dedication | 1 |
| Dedication and Acknowledgements | 3 |
| Foreword | 5 |
| A Letter From A Dear Friend | 7 |
| Introduction | 10 |
| 1. Scenes From My Window | 16 |
| 2. The Arrival | 30 |
| 3. Adolescence | 42 |
| 4. Glimmer of Hope | 54 |
| 5. The Fall | 77 |
| 6. The Breakthrough | 102 |
| 7. Holy Identify | 138 |
| 8. Full Circle | 158 |
| 9. Closing Reflections | 170 |
| About the Author | 195 |

# Special Dedication

**T**o the dreamers,

To the immigrants who traverse oceans with hope in their hearts and courage in their steps,

To the students who carry the weight of two languages and two worlds,

To the educators who light the path of knowledge with unwavering faith,

And to all who dare to rise above the shadows to embrace their divine purpose. This book is for you. May these pages resonate with your struggles, your triumphs, and your dreams. Like a glowstick that must be broken to shine, know that every crack, every trial, and every moment of breaking is not your end—it is the source of your brilliance. As Emma Lazarus etched timelessly onto the Statue of Liberty: *"Give me your tired, your poor, your huddled masses yearning to breathe free."* This dedication echoes her call—not just as a sanctuary for the weary, but as a celebration of resilience, transformation, and the light that emanates from within. In a world fractured by division, this is a tribute to those who rebuild bridges with love, to those who push forward despite the odds, and to those who rise—not just for themselves, but for others who follow. May you find in these words the courage to rewrite your story, the strength to rise from the ashes, and the faith to believe that your life is a masterpiece in the making. With unwavering hope and gratitude,

**Marcelo Sousa**

# Dedication and Acknowledgements

In the tapestry of existence, where every thread weaves a story of divine purpose, I bow in humble gratitude to the magnificent Creator who breathes life into every dawn. Through valleys of shadow and peaks of triumph, His grace has been my North Star, my very heartbeat.

To Jacqueline, my soul sister in Christ, whose unwavering spirit has danced alongside mine since the first chapter of this journey began. To my beloved New Jersey family, whose faith burned bright like eternal flames, illuminating the vastness of God's grand design when my own vision faltered.

To you, dear reader, seeking a beacon of hope in these pages—may you find not just a flicker but a blazing torch to light your way. And to every soul who has crossed my path, whether for a moment or a lifetime, you've left footprints on my heart that have shaped this narrative.

Like an ancient oak that whispers stories through its rings, each soul mentioned here has become part of my living testimony. Watch how it stands, defiant against storms, its roots anchored in faith's fertile soil, while its crown reaches toward heaven's infinite embrace.

These precious souls are the hidden architecture of my existence. Like the intricate network of roots beneath the earth's surface, they've held me steady when winds of doubt howled and waters of tribulation rose. Though invisible to the casual observer, their strength flows through every fiber of my being.

In life's fiercest tempests, these anchors of faith and love have kept me rooted in truth. Yet before any root took hold, the Master Gardener himself planted this seed with divine purpose, nurturing it with the waters of grace and the sunshine of mercy.

Through seasons of drought and moments of abundance, when branches hung heavy with sorrow or stretched bare against winter skies, Heaven's light never dimmed—even when my own inner flame flickered faintly in the darkness.

Though planted in soil often harsh and unyielding, this tree has flourished beyond mortal expectation, bursting forth in a symphony of growth and grace—a living testament to the Creator's artistry, the steadfast foundation of loved ones, and the eternal light of divine love. These beautiful souls are both my earthly anchor and my celestial light, illuminating paths yet untraveled.

To each precious heart to whom these pages are dedicated: you are the first brushstrokes on this canvas of grace. Whether you've walked beside me since the dawn of this journey or joined its unfolding chapters more recently, your presence has painted colors into my world that I never knew existed.

Through your love, wisdom, and sometimes even your challenges, you've helped forge these words that now flow forth to touch other hearts. Each of you holds a verse in this symphony of redemption, and my gratitude echoes through every page, every word, and every breath.

# Foreword

Identity, life, death, peace, sadness, and the pursuit of truth is a journey we are all walking. Every time the mirror looks back at us, we are reminded of a deep-seated need for value and purpose.

Meeting Marcelo in 2020 was one of the serendipitous moments in a long career of countless breakfasts with countless people. We immediately knew we were in for a great visit that morning and possibly the beginning of a lifelong friendship. That breakfast gave me a peek into a life story everyone needed to hear and share. Smart, funny, and even humble, Marcelo captivated me with his tale of a boy from Brazil. This book is essential for anyone who is winning or losing. That's why it's not optional reading but a must. Simply put, Marcelo matters—and so do you. Dive in.

Over the last twenty-nine years I have been working with kids, teens, men, women, families, and those who wrestle with addiction. One common thread is that identity matters for healing, reconciliation, and living on mission. If one cannot identify who they are and whose they are, much confusion and sadness follow. Helping a person connect to their Creator is the greatest healing we offer one another. As we begin to identify as a creation that is loved by our Maker, value and purpose easily follow.

I am thankful Marcelo has not offered us a book about being a better version of himself or even the best version of himself. He is a resurrected man, born again through the fires of trial and mercy. He has crafted a faithful narrative of what is possible when God collides with a human.

Pastor Steven J. Kiley
Evangel Chapel Clinton

# A Letter From A Dear Friend

My Cherished Soul Friend,

My heart swells as I write these words, for I am so proud of you and deeply moved by this achievement. Your journey reminds me of the eternal dance of the moon across our night sky. You went through myriad phases in your life, but just like the celestial guardian hanging impossibly distant yet intimately close, no earthly force can change God's divine blueprint for you.

Through your darkest nights, when shadows of doubt eclipsed your spirit and despair threatened to extinguish your light, you persevered. But you are just like the moon—your luminescence, borrowed yet brilliant, cannot be diminished by mortal hands. It flows from the very heart of God. Like our faithful lunar companion, continue to orbit in His presence, for He is the sun of justice that bathes creation in endless radiance. May His glory continue to cascade through your being.

As the moon's gentle pull orchestrates the ocean's eternal dance, your words shall touch and transform the lives of others. May the splendor of Jesus kindle an ever-brightening flame within your soul. May this divine radiance overflow and embrace all those around you.

Step forth into your calling, wrapped in heaven's light like a cloak of stars. I wish you an abundance of divine presence, where each heartbeat echoes God's promises, and every step reveals His perfect peace. These are the whispered prayers of my heart for you, my friend, whom I cherish beyond measure.

In the love of Christ Jesus, I echo His timeless commission: 'Go into all the world, preach the gospel to every creature' (Mark 16:15). Like the moon that faithfully illuminates the darkness, may you light the way for others seeking His truth.

With deepest affection and eternal hope,

Jacqueline Oliveira de Jesus Silva

# THE BOY FROM BRAZIL

# Introduction

## Moments of Impact

*My life has been been defined by a series of moments of
impact. Moments I've felt collide with me at such force they've reshaped
my entire identity. Moments that unapologetically burnt my world, as
I knew it, to the ground, leaving me to sift through the ashes.
Each and every time I felt the ground stop shaking, I'd find myself with
a paintbrush in my hand, recreating the image of who I was. As I gaze
upon the canvas in front of me, I see the significance of each brush stroke-
I see depth, I see character, I see wisdom, I see experience, I see growth, I
see humility, I see empathy, but most importantly, I see these moments
of impact stroke by stroke creating a more beautiful me.*
-CindyCherie

L ike a window into another world, the postcard trembled in my
young hands, its painted landscape shimmering with possibility.
From the window of my mind, mansions rose like castles in the mist,
like nothing I'd ever seen before. Time crystallized in early November
1988, when this fragment of America arrived from my father, a paper
bridge across oceans. There it stood: the angelic white church on the

hill, crowned with foliage that blazed like stained glass, illuminating the beauty of what I thought heaven must be like. Peace descended like morning dew—a simple assurance of the future place that God had created for me. This eternal dwelling stretched beyond the boundaries of my childhood dreams, vast as the Brazilian sky yet intimate as a prayer. Not myth but miracle; not fantasy but sacred ground. It was something to look forward to. Like a compass needle finding true north, my soul aligned with the knowledge that transformation beckoned. I had no idea that it was all part of God's plan, a journey filled with many unexpected turns.

Brazil instilled in me a sense of unbridled curiosity, as wild as the Amazon itself. Hours would dissolve as I tracked butterflies' aerial ballet, their wings painting stories across the tropical air, and how God designed such beautiful wings and patterns. Dreams wove through my consciousness like golden threads, while compassion beat steady as a heart within me. My imagination didn't merely color my childhood—it architected entire universes. Reality bent and shifted beneath my touch as I conjured worlds within worlds. Each day brought new realms to explore and new stories to inhabit. I have this vivid memory of being six years old, perched like a curious sparrow in the car's front seat, my questions sprouting like spring leaves, and never being satisfied with quick answers. I possessed a profound spiritual understanding that transcended my own comprehension, truly transcending this world.

At seven, destiny led me through ancient wooden doors beside my mother into a sanctuary that would forever alter my path. The church's soaring architecture reached toward heaven like a stone prayer, drawing an involuntary smile of wonder across my face. The tower on the building, topped by a slender, pointed end, pierced the sky like a holy needle threading earth to heaven. Upon entering, the air itself seemed to part like a celestial curtain, revealing a presence that wrapped around me like a warm embrace—something ancient yet new, vast yet intimate.

These words pulse from my heart like healing waters, meant to nourish parched souls. Though I claim no mastery of the written word, tears baptize these pages as my pen traces the contours of memory. I don't know how many pages this book will be, but know this: if these words can kindle even a single smile, illuminate one darker path, or whisper hope into a silent moment, then they will have served their sacred purpose. My story can be related to the Parable of the Prodigal Son. Like that ancient tale, it winds through darkness before bursting into the light of redemption and jubilation. It is in our brokenness that we can find our roadmap to healing. God's voice echoes through our fractures: curious as a child's question, gentle as morning light, and surprising as spring rain.

Within these pages lies the chrysalis of identity—the sacred struggle of metamorphosis from what was to what could be. Watch as loneliness and guilt dissolve like morning mist, revealing a landscape painted in love's infinite hues. I have always longed for something more but didn't know what it was. It all began with the want. These words flow first as a healing balm for my own soul. To that little boy from Brazil who never stopped dreaming and who always, and still does, has an enormous heart. Each page unfolds like a key, revealing doors to the possibilities of tomorrow.

The journey from Brazil to America stretched wider than oceans, deeper than language, and higher than culture. It has also been unfathomably rewarding. I sometimes wonder how my life would have been different if I had stayed in Brazil. And then I catch myself. The future beckons like a lighthouse through fog, while the past whispers like distant waves. Does the butterfly yearn for its cocoon, or does

# THE BOY FROM BRAZIL

he envision soaring through the skies and indulging in the delectable nectar of life?

Raw truth will pulse through these pages like lifeblood. I want to have a conversation with you about change and love. Let us speak in the language of grace, where bitterness finds no purchase. For me, I found a solution where darkness was banished by light. I now fully understand that God is the embodiment of love on earth.

The mark of a Christian is our love for God, the world, and our neighbor.

May these words serve as a beacon of hope for those who journey alone. All of us need to stand up for the oppressed. Countless nights, isolation wrapped around me like a shroud; identity became a cage of my own making. I never desired to disrupt the status quo and consistently adhered to the norm. Mediocrity offered a comfortable mask, normalcy a safe harbor in stormy seas.

What I learned later in life was that it takes courage to be different. It takes courage to be successful. It takes courage to win. Years of searching crystallized into a moment of liberation as authenticity finally shattered the chains of conformity. I learned that God is present in our broken stories. He invites us to reflect on where we have come from so that we can join Him in where we are supposed to go.

Let these pages dissolve the distance between us, creating an intimate dialogue of hearts. The story is deeply personal, one I would share with family and friends. So welcome, dear reader. Settle in, dear friend, with your chosen comfort—perhaps the aromatic embrace of coffee or the gentle wisdom of tea steaming in your favorite mug—and picture yourself sitting with me on your porch. Nature orchestrates a perfect symphony: birdsong carries on the wind, butterflies dance their silent ballet, and here we sit, two souls sharing one story.

Life unfolds like an imperfect tapestry, beautiful in its very flaws. There are always twists and turns along the way that you never anticipated. At times, you will weep, and that is okay. It is all part of the deal. Pain carves the channels through which success later flows. We must analyze life when it knocks us down. In my darkest moments, I learned to transmute pain into purpose, allowing suffering to sculpt a stronger, wiser self. So, take a gulp of your drink of choice, sit back, and let me take you on the journey of my life.

# THE BOY FROM BRAZIL

# Chapter 1

---

# Scenes From My Window

*"Love is patient, love is kind. It does not envy, it does not boast, it is not proud, it is not rude, it is not self-seeking, it is not easily angered, and it keeps no record of wrongs. Love does not delight in evil but rejoices with the truth."*

*1 Corinthians 13: 4-6*

Like a whispered prayer made visible, the butterfly emerged from nowhere, ascending through shafts of golden light that pierced the Brazilian morning. Its wings, painted with nature's finest brushstrokes, commanded stillness from all who witnessed its dance, influenced by the sources of light and energetic currents flowing all around. Each beat of its wings seemed to conduct an invisible symphony, conducted by the choir of the heavens, following in rhythmic vibrations. Time itself seemed to pause as it pirouetted through the air, each movement a testament to both fragility and determination.

THE BOY FROM BRAZIL                    17

Landing on a single red rose, it unfurled its wings like pages of an
ancient story, each pattern a chapter, preparing to tell the story of a boy
who would one day share his plight with the world. In that moment,
divinity touched earth, confirming a message that God was always,
and will always, be nearby. Like a celestial sentinel, it embodied God's
watchful presence, wrapping me in wings of protection and whispers
of comfort. An emblem of a journey of change and growth. A story of
identity and dreams, and of a being that would one day reach his full
potential.

In a world spinning ever faster on its axis of uncertainty, I wandered
through decades like a sleepwalker, forty years passing like pages torn
from an unfinished novel. I speak to you with love and humility. Brazil
cradled my childhood in her warm embrace, weaving memories as
vibrant as her tropical flowers and as enduring as her ancient mountains. If you want to know my heart and who I truly am, you must
understand my childhood and where it all began.

## Where it All Began

In the heart of Minas Gerais, where mountains cradle the sky and
history whispers through colonial streets, I found my first home in
Belo Horizonte. Perched above a bustling bus depot on Rua Espinosa,
our apartment stood like a watchtower over a sea of urban motion,
where every passing footstep wrote a new line in the city's endless story.

Even now, decades later, I can close my eyes and hear the symphony
of the depot: the deep bass of idling engines, the percussive hiss of
air brakes, the rhythmic swoosh of brushes against metal as workers
prepared their mechanical charges for journeys into Brazil's vast unknown. These sounds were my lullaby, the heartbeat of my childhood
world.

Stories flowed as freely as diesel fuel beneath our home. My father, orchestrating the depot's daily dance from his administration office, created a space where every driver became family and every passenger carried tales from distant corners of our sprawling nation. The garage transformed into an impromptu theater, where road-weary travelers and seasoned drivers traded narratives like precious currency.

In this mechanical kingdom, I became its youngest citizen, a wide-eyed collector of stories, drinking in every word like sweet guaraná. Through my father's quiet wisdom and the kaleidoscope of perspectives shared by countless passing strangers, I learned to see the world not as a single story but as a tapestry of countless interwoven tales. Little did I know then how these early lessons in listening would shape the man I would become.

Faith bloomed early in my soul, taking root alongside the jacaranda trees that lined our streets. As the son of a missionary, I inherited not just beliefs but a lens through which to view the sacred in the everyday. While my mother dedicated her weekdays to missionary studies in the heart of the city, our weekends involved a different pilgrimage across town, where the renewed Presbyterian church awaited like a spiritual beacon.

Our Pentecostal sanctuary rose like a fortress of faith, nestled between the favelas and the undulating hills, occupying its own pocket of time and space. Though surrounded by the city's ceaseless pulse, it carved out a realm where the sacred and secular danced an intricate waltz, where heaven seemed to bend closer to earth.

The 1980s Pentecostal Fundamentalist world shaped me like a potter's hands on willing clay, molding beliefs that would both anchor and challenge me in the decades to come. In those formative years, divine conversation felt as natural as breathing—I spoke to God in whispers and shouts, and His responses echoed through the chambers

# THE BOY FROM BRAZIL

of my young heart. What began as simple childhood faith would eventually crystallize into something more complex and profound: a foundation for critical thinking and worldly engagement that my younger self could never have imagined.

In the shadow of my father's quiet leadership, I grew like a sapling reaching toward sunlight. He never delivered formal lessons in character or courage; instead, he led by example, each action a brushstroke in the masterpiece of my developing consciousness. Under his steady gaze, my confidence took root and flourished, nourished by the rich soil of his unwavering presence.

It wasn't until the passing of time and my personal struggles that I truly realized the extent of his impact. Like a master craftsman passing down ancient techniques, he had silently transmitted patterns of interaction and understanding that would become the blueprint for my own journey through life's intricate maze of relationships. His legacy lives on in every handshake, every conversation, and every moment of empathy I share with others—a living testament to the power of patient guidance and unconditional love.

## Peering Through the Window

My window became my portal to the universe, a crystalline lens through which the theater of life unfolded in endless acts. From my perch above the street, I watched humanity flow like a river beneath me—merchants with their weathered hands, students clutching dreams in worn backpacks, lovers sharing secret smiles. Each passing figure sparked stories in my seven-year-old imagination, tales that bloomed like wild orchids in the fertile soil of my mind. In that age of infinite possibility, every story I conjured felt as real as the warm Brazilian sun that filtered through my glass observatory.

Dawn broke one morning to the primal pulse of drums, their rhythms reaching through walls to pull me from sleep like invisible hands. Carnival—our southern Mardi Gras—had arrived in an explosion of sound and color. The celebration's heartbeat grew stronger, wilder, until it seemed to shake the very foundations of our building, its primitive power awakening both wonder and terror in my young heart.

Instinct drove me beneath my bed, where I curled like a frightened cat in my fortress of shadow, imagination painting monsters from the merrymakers below. However, the insatiable curiosity of childhood would not allow me to remain hidden for long. Something deeper than fear pulled me back to my window stage, where courage was rewarded with a vision of pure joy unleashed.

Below, a living river of turquoise flowed through the street—hundreds of bodies moving as one in costumes that captured the essence of sky and sea. Their garments rippled like waves beneath the sun, each sequin and feather a promise of prosperity, health, and joy. From my celestial balcony, I transformed from spectator to honored guest as the revelers looked up, their waves and smiles anointing me as part of their magnificent celebration.

Across the street, a massive tent unfurled like a butterfly's wings, its yellow and blue stripes announcing the arrival of the circus with all the grandeur of a royal proclamation.

From my aerial vantage point, I became both archivist and dreamer, each detail of the circus's birth etching itself into my memory like hieroglyphs on ancient walls. The rehearsals unfolded like chapters in a living storybook: painted clowns testing their laughs against the morning air, acrobats weaving invisible tapestries in space, and exotic animals padding through their paces with ancient dignity. As twilight descended, music would spiral upward—a blend of brass and

# THE BOY FROM BRAZIL

percussion that painted the air with possibility. Deep into the night, motorcycle engines would growl their mechanical symphony, their riders tracing dangerous patterns in the darkness, preparing to defy death for the price of admission.

Yet my window also framed darker tableaux, none more haunting than the daily appearance of a woman who seemed to wear tragedy like armor. She would emerge from the morning mist like a character from a forgotten story, her black clothing a stark contrast against the colorful Brazilian street life. Her movements were a strange dance—part defiance, part despair—as she carved her daily path through the crowd, which parted before her like waves before a dark ship. The massive black sack she carried seemed to contain all the world's sorrows, and her incomprehensible shouts rang out like prophecies no one could decode. Through my young eyes, she appeared both fearsome and fascinating—a lost soul who had perhaps once known grace, now raging against a world that had forgotten her name. Her presence imparted to me my initial lessons about the shadows of life and the delicate boundary between belonging and exile. Even now, decades later, I find myself wondering what stories that black sack contained, what circumstances had written such a harsh ending to what must have once been another little girl's hopeful beginning.

## Memories with My Father

In the tapestry of my childhood memories, my father's thread weaves golden and strong, a constant that held our family's fabric together. Each morning began like a sacred ritual: prayers whispered in the pre-dawn quiet, then the descent to his white pickup truck—our chariot to the day's adventures. Although the cab was not designed to accommodate a family of four, this limitation turned out to be a hidden blessing. Standing behind the seats, my small hands gripping my father's shoulders, I found my place of belonging. Each bump in the road, each turn through the awakening streets of Belo Horizonte, bound me closer to him. In those moments, pressed between sky and earth, I learned what it meant to trust completely, to be protected unconditionally. These weren't mere school runs; they were daily lessons in love, written in the language of presence and touch, archived forever in the vault of my heart.

The vast parking lot of the Mineirao stadium became my proving ground, where at five years old, I faced the ultimate challenge of childhood independence. Against the backdrop of Brazil's largest football arena, my father orchestrated my transformation from earthbound child to two-wheeled adventurer. His hands steady on the bicycle seat, his voice a gentle current of encouragement—"Keep "pedaling, keep pedaling"—he" became both anchor and wind beneath my wings. The expanse of asphalt stretched before me like an endless sea, each attempt at turning a battle against gravity and fear. My knees accumulated scrapes, serving as badges of courage, and each fall taught me that pain was simply the cost of progress. Through frustration and fatigue, his unwavering presence reminded me that some victories are won not in single moments of triumph but in the stubborn refusal to surrender. When mastery finally came, his cheers echoed off the stadium walls, a sound sweeter than any World Cup roar.

Weekends brought pilgrimages to Lake Pampulha, where nature created her masterpiece on the opposite side of our bustling city. The approach itself was a gradual awakening: first the wild abundance of vegetation guarding the lake's entrance like emerald sentinels, then the sudden reveal of waters so still and clear they seemed to hold the sky in their depths. These journeys became our family ritual—windows down, Brazilian air rushing through the cab, carrying the mingled

# THE BOY FROM BRAZIL

scents of water lilies and adventure. Along the shoreline, vendors created a marketplace of dreams: rainbow-hued kites dancing on display, hand-woven hammocks swaying like pendulums marking lazy time. Here, astride my now-mastered bicycle, I would drift through afternoon reveries, my thoughts as fluid as the lake itself. Nature's symphony—water lapping at the shores, leaves whispering secrets to the wind—became the soundtrack to my growing understanding of peace.

Certain Sundays were reserved for our pilgrimage to the airport, where earth and sky conducted their eternal dance of farewell and reunion. From our perch on the observation deck, my father and I became witnesses to humanity's endless cycle of departure and return. Below us, travelers flowed like tributaries joining a river, each carrying stories and dreams in their wake. The thunder of jet engines trembled the air, each takeoff a defiance of gravity that ignited my imagination. My father, ever the patient teacher, would unfold the mysteries of flight for me—each aircraft type a character in an ongoing story, every airline livery a flag from distant realms I yearned to explore. We tracked flight paths like astronomers charting celestial bodies, finding peace in the metronomic rhythm of landings and departures. In this sacred space above the terminal, where time moved to the pulse of aviation, I discovered that sometimes the greatest adventures begin simply by watching others embark on theirs.

## My Childhood Shaped Me

I had an amazing childhood. These memories were essential to my development. I learned what it meant to be happy. How children absorb, understand, respond, and react to their environment are all critical factors in how their adult life will unfold, like the wings of a beautiful butterfly. It makes me happy to see families spending quality time together. Those were the moments that meant everything to me as a child, making me feel safe, secure, and loved. I would like you, dear reader, to go walk away from this chapter understanding that no one's childhood is perfect. For all of us out there caring for these little ones, all we can do is be there for our children as best we can and create a loving and safe environment for them to grow and develop into mature, happy adults. We serve as their safe haven until they are ready to take on new challenges.

Our life in Minas Gerais was punctuated by journeys to Ouro Preto, a city that seemed to have been carved from dreams and gold dust. Nestled in the ancient embrace of the Serra dos Espinhaco mountains, this 17th-century marvel stood as a testament to human artistry and divine inspiration. Here, the Baroque architecture transcended mere stone and mortar, with each building danced with light and shadow, its curves and flourishes defying the very notion of walls as barriers. The city unfolded like a living poem: golden churches reaching toward heaven, cobblestone streets that whispered centuries-old secrets, and windows that caught the sun like diamonds in the mountain air.

Walking those undulating streets with my parents, I witnessed how the changing light transformed each façade into a different masterpiece hour by hour. The way sunbeams caressed the ornate details of churches and mansions awakened something profound within me—a nascent understanding that beauty could be both mathematical and mystical. This was more than an introduction to art; it was an initiation into the sacred language of creativity itself. Each visit planted seeds of wonder that would bloom into a lifelong passion for artistic expression, teaching me that the greatest masterpieces are those that continue to reveal new depths with each encounter.

## THE BOY FROM BRAZIL                                    25

Then came the pivotal moment in second grade when the theater claimed my heart. The house lights gave way to darkness, and the curtain, like a magician revealing his greatest trick, drew back, ushering me into a realm of limitless possibilities. The actors before me were more than performers—they were alchemists, transforming mere words into living, breathing moments of truth. Though modest in scale, this production wielded the power of pure magic, igniting a spark in my soul that would grow into an eternal flame.

My initial experience with live theater served as a gateway to explore the infinite realms of my imagination. In that sacred space where reality and dreams intertwined, I discovered the beauty of life's ambiguities, the power of standing in someone else's truth. Each subsequent performance I witnessed became another brick in the foundation of my creative spirit, building a sanctuary where experimentation flourished and risk-taking became an act of joy rather than fear.

Looking back through time's gentle lens, I realize I was blessed with a childhood that sparkled with moments of pure magic. These weren't just memories, but foundational stones upon which my entire being was built. Through each experience—from the humble bus depot to the grandeur of Ouro Preto—I learned the intricate choreography of happiness. Like a butterfly emerging from its chrysalis, each interaction with my environment shaped the person I would become, every experience another brushstroke on the canvas of my developing soul.

Dear reader, as you close this chapter, understand that perfection in childhood is a myth as ethereal as morning mist. What matters is the presence of love, the steady hand of guidance, and the warm embrace of security. We who shepherd young souls through their early years are not tasked with creating flawless lives but with weaving protective cocoons of understanding and acceptance. Within these sacred spaces, our children gather strength for their eventual flight into the vast sky of adulthood, their wings colored by the memories we help create.

The tapestry of childhood weaves itself into the very fabric of our being, its patterns emerging in every choice we make, every path we choose. While not deterministic, these early experiences cast long shadows into our adolescent years, their influence as subtle as moonlight yet as powerful as ocean currents. It is in this crucial period that parental involvement becomes not just important but transformative—a force that can either nurture wings or clip them.

Children, with their minds and hearts absorbing life's lessons with the thoroughness of morning dew collected on a spider's web, are nature's most perfect apprentices. They learn not just from our carefully chosen words, but from the silent poetry of our actions, the unconscious grace or tension in our movements, and the hidden meanings in our pauses. The dissonance between our words and actions creates fault lines in their understanding, causing tremors that can undermine their foundation of trust.

Time spent with children is not merely measured in hours but in the depth of presence we offer. Every genuine moment of connection weaves into their emotional journey, from their first steps to their first failures, from whispered bedtime stories to triumphant bicycle rides. Like master gardeners, parents cultivate confidence through the fertile soil of encouragement, the warm sunshine of affirmation, and the gentle rain of earned praise. Yet this garden must allow for both growth and stumbling; children denied the chance to test their wings in the winds of challenge often find themselves earthbound by fear in later years. Self-esteem, a precious flower of childhood, requires both careful nurturing and the freedom to navigate life's challenges.

History offers us a stark mirror reflecting the power of childhood experiences in shaping humanity's leaders. Consider the contrasting

# THE BOY FROM BRAZIL 27

paths of Abraham Lincoln and Joseph Stalin, two individuals whose early years carved vastly different channels for their influence to flow. Lincoln, though touched by early loss, found nurture in his stepmother's gentle encouragement of his intellectual curiosity. Like a young tree reaching toward light through forest shadows, his love of learning flourished despite hardship, eventually growing into the wisdom that would heal a divided nation. Stalin, by contrast, emerged from a crucible of violence and betrayal, where love was twisted into control and tenderness hardened into brutality. The seeds of compassion, never properly nurtured in his childhood garden, withered into the thorns of tyranny that would later pierce millions.

Both men wielded immense power, yet one chose to break chains while the other forged them. The divergence of their paths can be traced back to those crucial early years, where character is molded like clay in the hands of circumstance and care.

The echoes of childhood reverberate through the chambers of destiny, shaping not just individual lives but the very course of human history. For parents and future parents alike, this understanding carries both profound responsibility and sacred opportunity. In nurturing our children with divine love, we plant seeds that may bloom into gardens of compassion or forests of wisdom. Yet mere exposure to spiritual teachings is not enough; we must embody the virtues we wish to instill, knowing that our actions write the first draft of our children's understanding of both earthly and heavenly love.

## Points for Reflection

1. What moment from your childhood still glows like a lantern in your memory, illuminating all that came after?

2. If time were a door you could open, which childhood scene would you step back into, and what wisdom would you gather there?

3. What childhood misstep, once a source of burning shame, now serves as a gentle teacher of humility and growth?

4. In the sacred dance of parenting, what steps do you believe are most crucial for guiding a child toward their fullest potential?

# Chapter 2

---

# The Arrival

*"Behold, I am with you, and I will keep you wherever you go and will bring you back to this land. For I will not leave you until I have done what I have promised you."*
*Genesis 28:15*

### My Street

I'll go but I'll return to see you again
But wait—let me memorize this moment...
Goodbye to the morning symphony of footsteps on cobblestone
Goodbye to bus engines humming their dawn prayers
Goodbye to mechanics' whistles echoing through open garage doors
Goodbye to pão fresh from the oven, steam rising like morning mist
Goodbye to sunlight dancing on lake waters, weekends stretched like
taffy
Goodbye to Sundays heavy with afternoon heat and family laughter
Goodbye to the friend who knows my heart's every secret
Goodbye to my Portuguese, the language that taught my tongue to
dance

## THE BOY FROM BRAZIL

Goodbye to laughter that bounces off walls like musical notes
Goodbye to feijoada that tastes like childhood memories
Goodbye to wheels spinning stories around the stadium's curves
Goodbye to church ladies with their knowing smiles and gentle blessings
Goodbye to cobblestones that have memorized my footsteps
Goodbye to the simple rhythms that became my heartbeat
Goodbye to windows-down drives through streets I know by heart
Goodbye to pipas painting the sky with rainbow dreams
Oh Brazil, you've carved yourself so deep in my heart.
Each goodbye leaves an echo that will call me home again.
Ok God, I'll go—but keep this piece of my heart safe until I return
See you soon...


### Minha Rua

Eu vou mas voltarei para te ver novamente
Mas espere—deixe-me memorizar este momento...
Adeus à sinfonia matinal de passos nas pedras portuguesas
Adeus aos motores dos ônibus entoando suas preces da madrugada
Adeus aos assobios dos mecânicos ecoando pelas portas abertas das oficinas
Adeus ao pão quentinho do forno, vapor subindo como névoa da manhã
Adeus à luz do sol dançando nas águas do lago, fins de semana esticados como caramelo
Adeus aos domingos pesados de calor e risos em família
Adeus à amiga que conhece todos os segredos do meu coração
Adeus ao meu português, a língua que ensinou minha língua a dançar

Adeus às risadas que ricocheteiam nas paredes como notas musicais
Adeus à feijoada que tem gosto de memórias de infância
Adeus às rodas girando histórias nas curvas do estádio
Adeus às senhoras da igreja com seus sorrisos conhecidos e bênçãos
gentis
Adeus às pedras portuguesas que memorizaram meus passos
Adeus aos ritmos simples que se tornaram meu batimento cardíaco
Adeus aos passeios de carro com as janelas abertas por ruas que conheço de cor
Adeus às pipas pintando o céu com sonhos coloridos
Ah Brasil, você se entranhou tão fundo no meu coração. Cada adeus
deixa um eco que me chamará de volta.
Ok Deus, eu vou—mas guarde este pedaço do meu coração até eu
voltar
Até logo...

Like a seed torn from fertile soil and cast onto foreign ground, I found myself transplanted into a culture that stripped away everything familiar, leaving me raw and exposed. Each day unfolded like a puzzle written in an alien language, its pieces refusing to fit together no matter how I turned them. For nine years, Brazil had been the canvas of my childhood, painted with the vibrant colors of mango trees and morning markets. Now, America loomed before me like a blank page, waiting to be filled with unfamiliar words and foreign rhythms.

Life shapes us like water shapes stone—gradually, relentlessly, until we emerge transformed. These watershed moments carve rivers through our identity, creating new channels through which our future must flow. In 1989, my identity shattered like a mirror dropped on concrete, each fragment reflecting a different version of who I thought

## THE BOY FROM BRAZIL

I was. Only later would I understand that sometimes we must break apart to be rebuilt stronger, like a bone that heals more resiliently at the point of fracture.

The sky hung low that afternoon, heavy with unspoken good-byes and the weight of impending change. My hands trembled as I buttoned my shirt that morning, each click of plastic through fabric counting down to departure. Deep in my bones, I felt the weight of what was coming—a journey measured not in miles but in heartbeats and tears.

Brazil wasn't just my home—it was a tapestry of precious moments I'd never see again: the window frame that had become my personal stage for watching the world, the circus that painted my neighborhood in weekly splashes of magic, the mysterious lady with her eternal black sack who always smiled as she passed. Each goodbye was a thread pulling loose from the fabric of my life: my best friend's laughter, the sweet warm scent of the bakery next door, the lullaby of buses orchestrating their daily dance, those sacred Sunday pilgrimages to Pampulia and the airport where dreams took flight.

That street—my street—would soon exist only in memory, its familiar rhythm fading like music carried away by wind, leaving behind an echo that would resonate in my heart for years to come.

The morning of our departure found me huddled in the corner of an emptying room, my questions bouncing off bare walls: Why? Why? Why? Each echo returned hollow, unanswered. The adults around me spoke of opportunity and the future, but their words were like distant stars—bright but impossibly far away, offering no warmth to a child's breaking heart. Voices swirled around me like autumn leaves in a storm, while my sister's eyes sparkled with the promise of adventure. But where she saw a door opening, I saw only a cage descending.

My roots were deeply ingrained in Brazilian soil, and the act of up-rooting felt like a violent act against the natural world. Yet somewhere beneath my despair bloomed a fragile flower of faith—a whispered promise that God's plan, like a garden in winter, would eventually reveal its purpose when spring returned.

The car door shut firmly, akin to the closure of a coffin lid. Through tears that transformed the world into watercolor, I pressed my face against the cool glass, trying to memorize every detail of home—the way sunlight caught the edge of the roof, the shadow of the mango tree, the familiar cracks in the sidewalk that had mapped my childhood adventures. Each sob was a prayer, each tear an offering to a God I believed could reverse time itself. But as the car pulled away, my prayers dissolved into the morning mist, teaching me my first harsh lesson about the immutability of certain goodbyes.

## The Anatomy of Farewell

Goodbyes are mirrors that reflect not just what we're leaving but who we are in the moment of leaving. They strip away pretense, leaving us naked before our own truth. Like a butterfly emerging too soon from its chrysalis, I was thrust into a world my wings weren't ready for, still soft and vulnerable, the wind a threat rather than a promise.

In the depths of my childhood theology, I clung to one certainty: that God's hand cupped around me like a shell around a pearl, that I was more than just stardust scattered by chance across the universe. Divine fingerprints marked my soul, each heartbeat echoing with the rhythm of unconditional love—even when that love felt as distant as the homeland I was leaving.

Through a child's eyes, I cradled that worn postcard from my father like a map to paradise, its glossy surface promising streets of gold and

# THE BOY FROM BRAZIL

skies of endless possibility. How strange that hope could fit in such a small rectangle of paper.

Reality, I would soon learn, has a way of developing differently than the pristine images we carry in our minds. That February morning in 1989, winter's teeth bit sharp and deep as we boarded the plane that would carry us across the equator, from summer to winter, from known to unknown.

My father's absence had carved a father-shaped hole in my world, and I ached to fill it with his presence again. The promise of reunion was the only star in my darkening sky, though even that light flickered with the static of conflicting emotions—love tangled with resentment, hope braided with fear.

America rose before us like a concrete forest, grey and imposing, nothing like the sun-drenched paradise promised in that dog-eared postcard. The gap between expectation and reality yawned wide enough to swallow all our carefully cultivated hopes. Disappointment crept in like frost, crystallizing into a kaleidoscope of darker emotions: anguish that painted my days in shades of grey, despair that whispered defeat into my dreams, guilt that wrapped around my throat like a scarf pulled too tight. My mind shifted into survival mode, instincts honed sharp as winter winds.

Houses crowded the streets like refugees huddled for warmth, their shoulders touching, their windows staring blank-eyed at the perpetual twilight of urban decay. They seemed to lean on each other, as if without their neighbors' support, they might collapse under the weight of collective desperation.

From my second-floor perch, the world outside had transformed from the gentle panorama of my Brazilian childhood into a harsh urban lightshow. Police sirens painted the night in alternating strokes of blue and red, their rhythm punctuated by the metallic symphony of handcuffs and the muffled drama of street-corner arrests.

Trains moaned their lonesome songs into the darkness, their steel wheels scribing endless figure-eights across the city's skin. Each whistle pierced the night like an arrow finding its mark in the empty chamber of my heart, where echoes of home used to live.

Memories of Brazil haunted me like phantom limbs: the rough embrace of my mango tree's bark, the rich aroma of feijoada simmering on Sunday afternoons, the languid peace of lakeside siestas. These treasures were already fading like photographs left too long in the sun, their colors bleeding into the grey American winter.

## Strangers in a Strange Land

I walked among them like a ghost carrying invisible luggage—each bag packed with the weight of displacement, each pocket stuffed with homesickness, every zipper straining to contain memories of a life they couldn't see. My window in Brazil had been a portal to possibility; here, windows were just glass eyes staring blindly at concrete horizons. In their faces, I read the word 'different' like a sentence, their sideways glances and whispered comments drawing borders around my otherness. Perhaps they were right—I moved through their world like a poem written in a language they couldn't read.

My thoughts spun like carousel horses, faster and faster, as I navigated the maze of inner-city education—a labyrinth of underfunding and overcrowding where dreams went to hide in dark corners. The school building rose before us each morning like a maximum-security prison fashioned from concrete and crushed aspirations. Its corridors twisted like intestines through the building's gut, eventually depositing me in what they euphemistically called the ESL classroom—a con-

## THE BOY FROM BRAZIL

verted broom closet where foreign tongues were meant to be tamed into submission.

Pain speaks a universal language. In my classmates' hollow eyes and worn shoes, I recognized fellow travelers on the road of hardship. We were a collection of young Atlas figures, each shouldering invisible worlds of poverty, family fractures, and unspoken traumas. Our backpacks carried more than books—they were weighted with the stones of broken dreams and the sharp edges of survival.

Education transformed into a survival game, with rules written in invisible ink and the referees having long since left the field. We were saplings trying to grow in concrete, while the system's bureaucratic machinery churned on, indifferent to our struggle for light and nurture.

Words swirled around me like angry wasps, their English stings sharp and bewildering. "¿Hablas español?" they asked repeatedly, as if all Latin American children emerged from the same linguistic cocoon. "Português," I would whisper back, but my correction evaporated in the air between us, unheard, unseen.

Every encounter with peers and adults contributed to my isolation, and every miscommunication added a layer to my self-doubt. The voices in my head grew louder than the ones around me, conducting a symphony of inadequacy that drowned out the music of learning. My knowledge transformed into a puzzle with missing pieces and gaps, echoing through my academic journey like footsteps in an empty corridor.

## The Art of Invisible Living

Existence evolved into a type of performance art, akin to a butterfly ensnared in a wind tunnel, its wings outstretched yet unfulfilled, ensnared in a never-ending cycle of survival devoid of meaning.

Each day's final bell echoed, serving as a constant reminder of my displacement. While other children rushed into their parents' embracing arms, I was collected by a neighbor—a woman whose kindness couldn't mask her stranger status, whose car felt like another form of exile.

My parents had become ghosts, their presence marked only by the echo of early morning departures and late-night returns. Mother's fingers grew calloused from feeding fabric through industrial machines, while Father's hands turned white with flour and weariness, kneading dough through double shifts that stretched like endless ribbons of time. The American Dream, I learned, smelled like industrial detergent and day-old donuts.

## Navigating the Waters of Change

Change strikes unexpectedly, challenging our comfort and adaptability. It creates a turbulence in the soul that no weather report can predict. In life's perpetual dance, change leads while we learn to follow, its rhythm the only true constant in our ever-shifting world. Like seasons turning or tides flowing, it moves through our lives with unstoppable momentum.

Change can occur suddenly, brilliantly, and transformatively. Whether it's a new assignment that disrupts our routine, a workplace that shifts beneath our feet, or an environment that transforms

# THE BOY FROM BRAZIL

overnight, we must learn to dance with uncertainty. Yet this dance often feels like learning new steps while the music is already playing, our feet stumbling to catch the beat of a different drum.

Change demands payment in the form of hours, dollars, and the valuable resource of human energy. Like travelers facing an unexpected detour, we instinctively resist the unfamiliar path, our minds calculating the cost of deviation from the known. Even the simplest changes ripple outward with unexpected consequences. Just as a car's maintenance demands both resources and patience, larger transformations in life require investments of spirit, will, and faith. Each shift, whether mechanical or metaphysical, carries its own price tag written in the currency of adaptation.

Change arrives like an eviction notice from our comfort zone, forcing us to pack up our familiar habits and move into unknown territories. Those who refuse to leave their comfortable corners risk becoming like fossils—preserved perfectly in their resistance, but no longer growing, no longer living. As the Earth spins on its axis, so too must we rotate through our own revolutions of growth and transformation. Stasis becomes a form of slow decay in a universe designed for perpetual motion.

Consider the cautionary tale of Kodak, once the undisputed monarch of photographic memory-making. Like a mighty oak that refused to bend with changing winds, this giant of industry stood rigid in its analog kingdom while digital storms gathered on the horizon. Their story unfolds like a developed photograph, revealing how even the mightiest can fall when they mistake their present success for future security. Though Kodak had once painted the world in colors of possibility, capturing life's precious moments on silver halide crystals, their resistance to digital evolution became their undoing. Like an overexposed photograph, their future slowly faded to white.

Change erodes our sense of control, akin to autumn winds removing leaves from trees, exposing us to the reality of our vulnerability. We cling to the illusion of control like a life raft in stormy seas, each wave of change threatening to pull us under. In our search for sanctuary, we grasp at earthly anchors—the steady hand of government authority, the promised security of corporate success, the familiar embrace of career achievement. Like children building sandcastles against the tide, we construct fortresses of presumed stability. Yet each fortress, no matter how carefully constructed, stands vulnerable before time's relentless waves, built on foundations as shifting as desert sands.

But rising above the temporal tumult stands an eternal lighthouse, its beam cutting through storms of uncertainty with unwavering constancy. In God's unchanging nature, we find the true north our spinning compasses seek. Hebrews 13:8's ancient words, "Jesus Christ is the same yesterday, today, and forever," resonate across centuries as a beacon of hope. In a world where even mountains erode and stars burn out, His constancy stands like an eternal cornerstone, His faithfulness flowing like an endless river even when our own faith runs dry.

His promises anchor themselves in the bedrock of eternity, offering solid ground beneath our feet whether we walk through valleys of shadow or dance on mountaintops of joy. These divine guarantees transcend our circumstances, their truth undiminished by our acceptance or denial.

Before this unchanging God, we stand like saplings reaching toward sunlight, our growth determined by how deeply we root ourselves in His eternal nature. As we intertwine our story with His, trust blossoms like spring flowers after winter's retreat, each petal serving as a testament to the beauty of divine constancy in a world of perpetual flux. In knowing Him, we finally begin to know ourselves—creatures of change learning to dance with the Unchanging One.

# THE BOY FROM BRAZIL

## Points for Reflection

1. Like the narrator's journey from Brazil to America, what profound transition has reshaped your life's landscape? How did this experience transform both your external circumstances and internal identity?

2. In your journey of faith, what familiar "windows" did you have to leave behind to embrace new perspectives through Christ?

3. Where do you find yourself standing between worlds, like the narrator?

4. In what ways has God's unchanging nature served as your lighthouse during storms of change?

# Chapter 3

# Adolescence

*"And the Lord said, 'Behold, they are one people, and they have all one language, and this is only the beginning of what they will do. And nothing that they propose to do will now be impossible for them."*
*Genesis 11:6*

### Growing Up

Blind to the radiance within his soul,
A fractured mirror shows half-truths untold.
The child within him weeps in shadowed halls,
Yearning to belong behind concrete walls.

No prescription heals his hidden pain—
In dark corners, he curls, contained.
His mind: a maze of dreams and fears,
In concrete towers, no roses near.

# THE BOY FROM BRAZIL

Where city shadows chase away
The dance of wings on summer days,
Behind sealed glass, he dims his light
With flickering screens and endless fright.

His universe shrinks to matchbox size,
Blind to the wings beneath his spine,
Divine reflection lost in haze—
A chrysalis of darker days.

Each teardrop falls like sacred rain
On dormant seeds of hope and change,
Divine designs lay hidden deep
In soil where future gardens sleep.

In twilight faith, he learns to rest,
Like flowers sensing nature's breath.
Patient for dawn's revealing light,
For wings to spread in sacred flight.

Through cycles of death and rebirth,
His spirit yearns for skyward mirth.
Though wrapped in solitude's cocoon,
In fragments small, night's darkest noon—

He rises now, a gradual grace,
Like dawn that paints the morning's face.
Ascending through the breaking day,
His wings unfold, he finds his way.

## Crescendo

Cego à radiância dentro de sua alma,
Um espelho partido mostra meias verdades sem calma.
A criança interior chora nos corredores sombrios,
Ansiando pertencer entre muros vazios.

Sem prescrição que cure sua dor velada—
No canto escuro, sua forma está curvada.
Sua mente: um labirinto de sonhos e medos,
Em torres de concreto, sem rosas nos arredos.

Onde sombras urbanas afugentam
O bailar das asas que ao verão sustentam,
Atrás do vidro selado, sua luz se apaga
Com telas piscantes e um medo que não vaga.

Seu universo encolhe ao tamanho de um grão,
Cego às asas sob sua própria construção,
Reflexo divino perdido na neblina—
Uma crisálida em dias que declina.

Cada lágrima cai como chuva sagrada
Sobre sementes de esperança guardada,
Desígnios divinos jazem ocultos, profundos
No solo onde jardins futuros são fecundos.

## THE BOY FROM BRAZIL

Na fé crepuscular, aprende a descansar,
Como flores que sentem a natureza pulsar.
Paciente pela luz que há de revelar,
Para asas em voo sagrado desdobrar.

Por ciclos de morte e renascimento,
Seu espírito anseia pelo firmamento.
Embora envolto no casulo da solidão,
Em fragmentos pequenos, na mais escura escuridão—

Ele se ergue agora, com graça gradual,
Como aurora que pinta a face matinal.
Ascendendo através do dia nascente,
Suas asas se abrem, encontra-se presente.

She emerged from the ether like a fragment of starlight given wings, her presence both delicate and divine. Her wings, iridescent and vast as cathedral windows, bore witness to creation's finest artistry. Time itself seemed to pause, caught in the cascade of light that poured through clouds and pierced the veil between earth and heaven. She danced through the air in rhythmic pulses, each wingbeat a note in nature's symphony, each movement a prayer written in motion. To the small boy below, whose path through darkness still lay ahead, she appeared as heaven's own messenger, bearing wisdom in her gossamer embrace.

"Child of stardust and earth, your life will unfold like a tapestry of light and shadow, each thread essential, each pattern sacred. In the whispers of your heart, you'll find God's voice guiding you. Your journey ahead is a solo flight through uncharted skies, where each current of wind carries both challenge and possibility. Know this: my prayers will follow you like invisible wings, and when you emerge transformed, I'll be waiting to witness the masterpiece of your becoming. Together, we'll inscribe your story in the book of life. Trust in this promise, dear one: even in darkness, you'll find your way. Now spread your wings, my kindred spirit, and claim the sky as your own."

Her gaze penetrated his very essence, and in that sacred moment, her crystalline tears reflected universes of understanding. Her mighty wings, now trembling like autumn leaves, betrayed the weight of foreknowledge. In the depth of her silence lay oceans of unspoken truth. Around her, reality began to fray at the edges, colors bleeding into the void like watercolors in rain. The heavens' symphony swelled, calling her home to southern skies. With one final, graceful ascension, she dissolved into the living tapestry of her kin, a thousand wings painting the sky in motion, leaving behind only the echo of divine promise.

## Poverty's Shadow and Childhood's Light

Poverty wrapped around our lives like a threadbare blanket, barely warming the edges of our existence. Our neighborhood stood in that gray area between desperation and dignity. The two-bedroom apartment became our fortress of necessity, its walls both shelter and prison as years stretched into memory.

But in the embrace of nearby woods, I found my sanctuary, my Brazil-in-exile. Each tree I scaled became a tower in my displaced kingdom, its branches reaching toward the same sky that stretched above my distant homeland. Astride my rusty charger of steel and rubber, I transformed our humble streets into Camelot's realm, where every puddle became a magical lake, every shadow a noble adversary.

Under my guidance, the neighborhood children became knights of a new Round Table, our playground democracy built on imagination and honor rather than wealth or status. We forged alliances on dirt paths and sealed pacts beneath maple trees, our fellowship as sacred as any in Camelot's halls.

The stories of Camelot, whispered to me in the warm Brazilian nights of my childhood, blazed eternal in my mind's eye, their magic undimmed by distance or time. Each memory sparkled like a star in the constellation of my past, guiding me through the darkness of displacement. My soul still swayed to the invisible rhythms of my homeland, each heartbeat a samba, each breath a whispered saudade.

In retrospect, I see how necessity birthed invention in my American childhood. Though my heart ached for Brazil with the intensity of first love, survival demanded adaptation, and imagination became my greatest ally.

Adolescence swept in like a tempestuous cloud, brimming with darkness and electrifying with potential. Thirteen marked the borderland between childhood's certainty and adulthood's mysteries, a no-man's-land of identity where every step felt like crossing quicksand. Time stretched like taffy in those years, and I existed in perpetual metamorphosis—a butterfly suspended between forms, wings still wet with possibility, trembling at the edge of flight.

My tears carved rivers through those years, each drop a question mark suspended in the air. The terrain of adolescence unfolded before me, replete with uncharted territories marked with challenging decisions: the shifting sands of friendship, the turbulent waters of sexuality, the mountains of identity, and the alluring lure of chemical escapes.

Insecurity wrapped around me like a second skin, every glance from others feeling like judgment, every mirror reflecting doubt. My questions echoed in an empty room—profound and painful inquiries met only by the hollow sound of their own asking. Each potential confidant turned out to be a fleeting illusion, disappearing as soon as they approached. I found myself stranded on an island of anonymity, desperately signaling to passing ships of attention with whatever flares I could ignite. In this desert of connection, lust blossomed like a poisonous flower, its beauty and deadly promise of fulfillment.

Our household stood like a fortress of rules, its walls built from unbending principles and reinforced by unwavering discipline. As the architect and guardian of this structure, my mother wielded authority in a manner that simultaneously protected and wounded. Each regulation was carved in stone, immutable as ancient law, their sharp edges cutting deep into my sense of self-worth. Love seemed conditional, trapped behind the bars of compliance.

Her faith stood like a wall between us, its mortar mingled with equal parts devotion and fear. Every step I deviated from her biblical blueprint widened the chasm between us, causing even our shared blood to feel as fragile as water. Through the fog of adolescent rebellion, I glimpsed her own battle—a mother trying to bridge the gulf between divine mandate and human desire, between the child she prayed for and the one who stood before her.

Like the prodigal son before me, I found myself drawn to the horizon, where freedom's siren song promised relief from the suffocating embrace of family doctrine. The world beyond our walls beckoned with possibilities that gleamed like fool's gold in the distance. Reality proved both less and more than I imagined—an empty theater whose elaborate illusions captivated even as they deceived.

In my isolation, I became both architect and prisoner of my own fortress, each brick mortared with shame and defiance. The thrill of rebellion offered temporary sanctuary—brief explosions of feeling that lit up my hollow spaces like emergency flares in the dark. This shadow realm welcomed all lost souls, a carnival of the disconnected where pain masked itself as pleasure. Through its smoke-filled corridors I wandered, my anger echoing off mirrored walls, each shout of rebellion returning as false comfort. In this self-made pantheon, I crowned myself divine, never realizing I was kneeling at an altar of illusions.

Lust infiltrated our teenage world like a fever, consuming reason and restraint. It became our cosmic center, a gravitational force pulling all thoughts into its orbit. The corridors of high school hummed with its electric current, each whispered secret a spark in the charged air. Lust and identity fused into an inseparable alloy, desire becoming as essential as breath. Its alluring melody assured satisfaction in a realm of emptiness, with each fleeting joy igniting a deeper yearning in its wake. I chased these phantom satisfactions like a moth drawn to destroying flame, each flight bringing me closer to combustion.

True love became a foreign language I could no longer speak; its vocabulary of selfless giving replaced by the crude dialect of desire. The pure mathematics of love—that sacred equation of giving without calculation—remained unsolvable in my confused heart. Love demands the courage of open hands, the strength to release control. It flows like a cleansing river, washing away conditions and calculations. It is the holy paradox where sacrifice becomes gain, where giving creates abundance.

I blindly navigated the labyrinth of lust, where every path led back to myself and every connection transformed into a transaction. In this maze of mirrors, I couldn't distinguish between those offering love's lamp and those carrying lust's torch. Like scattered notes seeking their original melody, my heart yearned for authentic connection while settling for echoes.

Time's patient lens eventually brought clarity, and in Christ's reflection, I recognized myself in Jeremiah's story—another young prophet confronting his own inadequacies in the mirror of divine calling. Like him, I stood at the crossroads of capability and doubt, where youth met purpose, where words met wisdom, where fear transformed into faith through the alchemy of trust.

A holy tension stretches between three points of an eternal triangle: the divine above, sin's gravity below, and my soul suspended between. This brokenness lives in us like a fault line, threatening to split our foundations with every tremor of temptation. The fracture lines run so deep they seem etched into our DNA—this perpetual urge to usurp divinity, to crown ourselves sovereign of our own small kingdoms. Each sin weaves its own web of deception; each lie distances us further from truth until we find ourselves wandering in a maze of our own making, the path to God obscured by shadows of our creation.

## Wings of Change: The Butterfly's Revolution

Consider the poetry of chaos theory: the ripples of a single butterfly's wingbeat, amplified across continents, birth storms on distant shores. My adolescence embodied this delicate chaos, each choice sending tremors through the timeline of my becoming. Every heartbeat was a wing-flutter of hope, each breath an attempt to stir the winds of change. I yearned to create storms of transformation, to summon hurricanes of love and fulfillment, but instead, I found myself in the midst of a different tempest.

In my frantic search for external light, I overlooked the divine spark already burning within. Time's patient lens has brought clarity: God's love preceded my existence, His image etched into my very essence like a watermark on precious paper. But teenage eyes are often blind to eternal truths. I was a master of surfaces, cultivating a garden of artificial charms while my inner landscape lay barren. Inside, I echoed

# THE BOY FROM BRAZIL                                51

like an empty cathedral, my soul's chambers vast and vacant. The journey to wholeness would unfold like a slow-blooming flower, each petal of self-discovery opening in its own sacred time.

Depression arrives like an uninvited shadow, darkening the corners of both secular and sacred spaces. Its questions echo in countless hearts: "Am I alone in this darkness? Is this normal?" Even the most devoted followers of Christ find themselves walking through these valleys, their faith tested by the weight of invisible chains. The American Psychiatric Association depicts depression as a clinical condition that casts a gray shadow over our emotions, thoughts, and actions. Yet within this clinical framework lies a profound truth: while depression may be a formidable adversary, it need not be a permanent companion.

Like a thief in the night, depression steals the vibrant hues from life's palette, leaving behind a monochrome world where joy becomes memory and passion turns to ash. It spreads its tendrils through both spirit and flesh, casting its pall over home and workplace alike. Depression's seeds take root in diverse soils: in the sterile halls of hospitals where mortality looms large, in the empty rooms of houses no longer called home, and in the hollow spaces left by those who have departed for heaven's shores. For some, melancholy flows through their family tree like dark sap, rising unbidden to the surface in each generation, a shadow inherited alongside eye color and height.

In this valley of shadows, we are all potential pilgrims. The crucial wisdom lies not in avoiding the journey but in preparing our souls for its trials. Ancient wisdom speaks through Proverbs 12:25, illuminating the path from darkness to light: "Anxiety in the heart of man causes depression, but a good word makes it glad." These words bridge millennia to touch our modern wounds. Anxiety coils around the heart like a serpent, its grip spreading fear and dread through our being. It whispers uncertainties into our quietest moments, turning peace to restlessness.

When control slips through our fingers like water, anxiety rises like a tide. Yet scripture offers an anchor: the power of a word spoken in love, a divine whisper that can part the waters of our despair. This "good word" manifests in many voices: in the gentle counsel of a friend who sees our worth when we cannot, in the trained wisdom of healers who help us navigate our internal storms. Yet above all these earthly voices rings the eternal Word, God's truth echoing through scripture like thunder across still waters.

Within scripture's sacred pages, we uncover a divine prescription for our anxiety: "Do not be anxious about anything, but in everything, by prayer and petition, with thanksgiving, present your requests to God. And the peace of God, which transcends all understanding, will guard your hearts and your minds in Christ Jesus" (Philippians 4:6-7). These words shimmer with promise, like stars piercing through storm clouds.

Scripture's daily bread nourishes not just the shepherds but the entire flock. Like morning dew on parched ground, these words refresh our spirits, strengthening our inner being as surely as physical sustenance fortifies our bodies. Consider Christ in the wilderness, His forty-day fast a testament to spiritual hunger's supremacy over physical need. When temptation circled like a desert vulture, He proclaimed the eternal truth: "Man shall not live on bread alone, but on every word that comes from the mouth of God" (Matthew 4:4). His words echo across time, a reminder that our deepest sustenance flows from divine springs.

In these sacred pages lies our daily armor against depression's shadows. When darkness threatens to overwhelm, these words stand as lighthouses on storm-tossed shores, reminding us that our God towers

# THE BOY FROM BRAZIL

above our trials. As Psalm 46:1 declares with unwavering certainty, "God is our refuge and strength, a very present help in trouble." This truth blazes like a sunrise through our darkest nights, transforming our valleys of shadow into pathways of purpose, our wounds into windows of wisdom, and our struggles into stories of salvation.

## Points for Reflection

1. Who do you trust the most when it comes to sharing your personal struggles, and why do you feel comfortable opening up to them?

2. When it comes to reading the Bible, what do you find most challenging or enjoyable, and how does it impact your understanding of its teachings?

3. What time of day do you feel most focused and connected to God, and how can you use that time to dedicate yourself to Bible reading?

# Chapter 4

---

# Glimmer of Hope

**Painted Smile**

Tears streak silver when the big top rises
In the mirror, a stranger's face becomes his truth
Beneath the greasepaint lies a fractured ghost
The audience demands his joy-like tribute
Each stroke of makeup buries yesterday's grief,
Layer by layer, he entombs his darkness deep.
Shadow hues of melancholy persist,
Staining his core like ancient inkUnder his eyes,
half-moons of ash remain
The residue of midnight's burning dreams,
Carved deep as fossil shadows in stone
Then comes the metamorphosis of hue:
Rose-pink bleeds passion into hollow cheeks,
Marigold yellow spins spring from fingertips,
Emerald whispers of distant jungle mists,
Azure wraps him in sky and ocean depths,

# THE BOY FROM BRAZIL

Lavender soothes like twilight's gentle breath,
And white—pure white—erases what came before,
A blank canvas promising redemption's dawnAtop it all,
his miniature hat presides,
Where an artificial butterfly performsIts endless dance of sparkle and
deceit—
Suspended in a moment's perfect lie

## Sorriso Pintado

Lágrimas riscam prata quando a lona se ergue
No espelho, o rosto de um estranho torna-se sua verdade
Sob a maquiagem jaz um fantasma fragmentado
A plateia exige sua alegria como tributo
Cada pincelada enterra a tristeza de ontem,
Camada por camada, ele sepulta sua escuridão profunda
Tons sombrios de melancolia persistem,
Manchando sua essência como tinta antiga
Sob seus olhos, meias-luas de cinzas permanecem
O resíduo dos sonhos ardentes da meia-noite,
Esculpidos profundos como sombras fósseis na pedra
Então vem a metamorfose das cores:
Rosa-rosado sangra paixão nas faces ocas,
Amarelo calêndula tece primavera das pontas dos dedos,
Esmeralda sussurra névoas distantes da selva,
Azul-celeste o envolve em céu e profundezas oceânicas,
Lavanda acalma como o sopro suave do crepúsculo,
E branco—puro branco—apaga o que veio antes,
Uma tela em branco prometendo a aurora da redenção

No topo de tudo, seu chapéu miniatura preside,
Onde uma borboleta artificial executa
Sua dança infinita de brilho e engano—
Suspensa na mentira perfeita de um momento

Thunder rolled through the auditorium—not from storm clouds, but from hundreds of hands clapping in unison. Each surge of applause swept over me, erasing years of uncertainty. In that moment, under the warm glow of stage lights, I felt the director's faith in me validated, her judgment transformed into victory.

As the house lights bloomed, I drank in the sea of smiling faces before me—sustenance more vital than bread or water. Behind my closed eyelids, memories flickered like an old film reel: the lost child, stumbling through American school corridors and drowning in a sea of incomprehensible English; the "slow" student, whose intelligence was trapped behind language barriers; the sheltered soul, suffocating within the confines of what my family called Pentecostal paradise.

Paradise—their word, not mine—was really a gilded cage, its bars forged from verses like Revelation 22:15: "But outside are dogs and sorcerers and sexually immoral and murderers and idolaters, and whoever loves and practices a lie." They called our church an ark of salvation, but it was more like a coffin: airless, confined, sealed against the light. We were all pressed together like dried flowers in a Bible, preserved but lifeless, viewing the world through the same narrow lens, breathing the same stale air.

But metamorphosis had already begun. Despite the whispered warnings—"It's too hard," "Only the most talented get leads," "Prepare for disappointment"—I had emerged victorious. More than elated, I was transformed. As I stood there on that stage, I felt the last remnants

# THE BOY FROM BRAZIL

of my cocoon dissipating, my wings finally unfolding, prepared to embrace the wind of possibility.

## Parental Control

My story begins in the mystical heat of Brazil, where my mother danced with shadows. She was a priestess of Macumba—a practice Christians whispered about as black magic, born from the fusion of African faiths that had crossed the ocean in slave ships' holds. In our small town, she was a figure of fascination and fear: a woman who painted herself in bold colors and wore her power like perfume. The air around our home was thick with incense and intention, marked by the rhythmic pulse of ritual drums and the final cries of sacrificial chickens. Her world was one of spirits and secrets, where every need had its price in blood or blessing.

Into this world of mysticism and shadow, I arrived broken—a fragile seedling struggling to take root. My body betrayed me from the start: immune system faltering, nerves misfiring, each breath a battle. The doctors spoke in whispers, marking my life expectancy in months rather than years. My mother, true to her beliefs, carried my failing body from ritual to ritual, offering increasingly desperate prayers to her dark spirits. But Macumba's powers, which had seemed so potent in matters of love and fortune, fell silent before my infant suffering.

Then came the knock that would reshape our destiny—Christian missionaries at our door, their faith as bright and insistent as the Brazilian sun. My mother, who had repeatedly turned them away, now found herself at the brink of despair. In that moment of profound insight, she made a deal with a God she had not yet encountered: she offered my life in return for her unwavering devotion. The deal was made with the fierce determination of a mother's love, her old beliefs crumbling like autumn leaves in her hands.

Witnesses viewed what transpired as a miraculous event. As strange hands rested on my fever-hot forehead and foreign prayers filled our incense-stained rooms, my failing body found its will to live. Like a withered plant finally receiving water, I began to thrive. The price of this miracle was steep: my mother shed her old self like a snake's skin, emerging as a zealous Pentecostal whose fear of damnation matched her former embrace of the mystical. Her flowing skirts and bold make-up gave way to modest dresses and bare faces; her once-wild spirit was now contained within rigid doctrine. Even my father, whose blood had run more whiskey than water, transformed—the bottle replaced by the Bible, his drunken songs becoming hymns of praise. Together, they rode the wave of the Jesus Movement, former flower children now bearing the cross, their liberation ironically becoming my cage.

Our next transformation came with the roar of jet engines, carrying us north to New Jersey—spiritual soldiers dispatched to save the souls of America. The irony was sharp as winter frost: we were meant to be missionaries, bearers of divine light, yet we lived like hermits in our theological fortress. Our church saw the United States as a wasteland of moral decay, but how could we tend this garden while refusing to touch its soil?

My mother's protective instincts, already heightened by my miraculous survival, crystallized into an impenetrable shield. My world narrowed to the dimensions of a church pew and a school hallway. My first glimpse of freedom, theater, was out of reach, but I managed to secure a smaller reward: permission to join the choir.

In those days, I was a ghost drifting through my own life, transparent and undefined. The church force-fed us their interpretation of Scripture like birds stuffing their chicks, but instead of nourishment,

I felt suffocation. Their words felt like stones in my throat, their certainties as heavy as lead. Every Sunday, every Wednesday, every revival meeting, the same message hammered home: conform, believe, obey. But beneath their thundering sermons, a quiet voice whispered of something more—a self waiting to be discovered, a song yearning to be sung.

## The Foreigner

Language became my first battlefield in this new world. Like most ESL students, I found myself waging daily war against an invisible enemy: the gap between thought and expression. Words that had once flowed like water now stumbled on my tongue, crystallizing into strange shapes. In Portuguese, I was whole—articulate, confident, alive. But English transformed me into a fractured version of myself, each sentence a puzzle missing crucial pieces.

High school loomed before me like a labyrinth, its corridors echoing with unfamiliar idioms and cultural references that slipped through my fingers like smoke. My un-American upbringing had left me doubly foreign—an outsider not just in language, but in experience. Fear became my constant companion, whispering doubts in two languages, each one amplifying the other until panic rose like floodwaters, threatening to drown whatever sense of self I had managed to preserve.

The whispers followed me through school hallways: "Learning disabled." "Cognitive delays." "Processing issues." These labels clung to me like shadows, making me question the very architecture of my mind. But when the tests came—clinical measurements of memory, phonemic awareness, and processing speed—the results shattered their assumptions like glass. My intellect wasn't broken; it was simply speaking a different language.

The irony of my situation cut deep: here I was, perfectly capable of complex thought, yet trapped behind a wall of translation. Every concept had to journey from English to Portuguese and back again, like light bouncing between mirrors, losing a fraction of its clarity with each reflection. My mind was a library where all the books had been suddenly scrambled, their contents intact but their organization thrown into chaos.

Then came the pivot point—that moment when my teachers' confusion turned to revelation. "Above average," they said, their tone tinged with surprise as they moved me from remedial classes to honors. Like a bird finally finding its wings, my academic life soared. Words began to flow, ideas crystallized, and the fog of confusion lifted. But this liberation was confined to school hours only. Beyond those walls, my world remained unchanged: an endless cycle of church services, Bible studies, and prayer meetings, as if my family feared that too much secular knowledge might undo my miraculous healing from years before.

## The Choir and Theater

Some lessons brand themselves into your soul, becoming part of your DNA. For me, it was a talk by Rick Lavoie called "When the Chips are Down." His words crystallized my struggle: he explained that self-esteem was akin to carrying a bag of poker chips through life's casino.

The popular kids—the quarterback with his perfect spiral, the cheerleader with her magnetic smile—they walked the halls with bags overflowing. When life dealt them a bad hand—a wrong answer in class, a fumbled response—they barely noticed the loss. Their wealth

## THE BOY FROM BRAZIL

of confidence cushioned every blow and made every failure bearable. They had the financial means to gamble, take risks, experience spectacular failures, and then laugh it off.

But for those of us playing with empty bags, every interaction was high-stakes poker. Each raised hand in class, each attempted conversation, and each stumbled English phrase felt like pushing our last chip into the pot. One wrong move, one mispronounced word, and we'd be emotionally bankrupt.

My mother, haunted by her own spiritual transformation, saw pride as a demon more dangerous than any she'd known in her Macumba days. She played the role of a strict dealer, quick to collect my chips but never dealing new ones. My father, like a ghost at the table, neither added to nor took from my dwindling stack. In this rigged game, while others built their fortunes in the currency of confidence, I was scraping by on spiritual pennies, counting each small victory like a miser counts coins, never quite having enough to ante up for the next round of life's endless game.

The theater department beckoned, its stage lights piercing the darkness of my confined world like a siren's song. Every time I passed those heavy auditorium doors, I felt the pull of belonging, of becoming, of transformation. But my mother's prohibitions stood like angel's flaming swords at the gates of this secular Eden. Theater, sports, and any pursuit that might draw my heart away from the narrow path—all were labeled as "worldly," spiritual landmines waiting to destroy my soul.

The irony of fundamentalist fear is its selective nature. My parents scrutinized every secular influence as if examining bacteria under a microscope—music was dissected for hidden messages, movies were screened for the slightest hint of worldliness, and friendships were vetted with theological precision. Yet they never considered that too much church might be its own form of poison, that spiritual force-feeding could lead to malnutrition of the soul. We were so busy building walls against the world that we forgot to build windows for the light to shine through.

Looking back now, with the clarity that only time and healing can bring, I see how this suffocating spirituality became the very thing that delayed my true identity in Christ. Like a plant grown in darkness reaching desperately for light, I was stretching toward something I couldn't name—authenticity, perhaps, or the freedom to be fully human while fully His.

Scripture makes a clear statement about parental authority, which is intricately woven throughout God's design. The fifth commandment's call to honor father and mother (Exodus 20:12) echoes through both testaments, reinforced by Paul's words in Colossians and Ephesians. Parents bear the sacred duty of spiritual guidance, commanded in Deuteronomy to weave God's truth into the very fabric of daily life.

Yet in the tapestry of biblical parenting, I've come to see a pattern often overlooked in fundamental circles: God's own parenting style. He gives us room to stumble, to question, to wrestle—like Jacob at the Jabbok River, fighting for his blessing. Divine love creates space for growth, for discovery, for the painful but necessary process of becoming. True identity in Christ isn't inherited like a family heirloom; it must be forged in the furnace of personal experience, shaped by both triumph and failure.

Like a gardener who pulls their seedlings too close, a parent's desperate grasp for spiritual control often chokes the very growth they hope to nurture. God's own example exemplifies this, standing at the door and knocking without ever breaking it down. He offers choice, extends invitations, and plants seeds but allows them to grow at their own pace. When we clutch our children too tightly, we risk crushing

# THE BOY FROM BRAZIL 63

their spirits like delicate flower petals in an anxious fist. True faith, like true love, must be chosen freely, nurtured in the open air of grace rather than the hothouse of fear

## Finding My Identity

The school's choir program stood like a fortress of excellence, its walls adorned with golden trophies and crystalline memories of perfect harmonies. In my freshman year, drawn by an inexplicable hunger for music, I made my first real act of courage: I decided to audition. My sister, love wrapped in thorny pessimism, tried to shield me from what she saw as inevitable disappointment. "Oh Marcelo," she'd sigh, her words heavy with protective doubt, "you're just a freshman. The concert choir? They're beyond good—they're exceptional. Don't set yourself up for heartbreak."

But something was stirring within me, a recognition that transcended her well-meaning warnings. Like a caterpillar sensing the approach of spring, I felt the first tremors of transformation. The process was so subtle at first, like the imperceptible hardening of a chrysalis, that few noticed the change beginning. Yet in those moments of preparation, standing before the mirror practicing scales, I began to understand the profound alchemy taking place in my soul.

Nature's wisdom whispered its truth: every butterfly must spin its own cocoon, must struggle alone in the darkness of transformation. There are no shortcuts in metamorphosis, no way to borrow another's wings. The process demands solitude, requires courage, and above all, insists on authenticity. In those days of preparation, I wasn't just learning music—I was learning the ancient art of becoming.

Inside my chrysalis of uncertainty, I couldn't yet measure the wingspan of my potential. But deep within, a spark had ignited—a tiny flame of possibility that grew stronger with each passing day, burning away the fog of doubt. Like all metamorphoses, mine demanded a leap of faith: that terrifying moment when the caterpillar must trust in its transformation, must believe in wings it cannot yet see or feel.

The choice crystallized before me with stark clarity: remain forever in the comfortable darkness of my cocoon or risk everything for the promise of flight. The voices around me—well-meaning family, cautious friends, my own persistent doubts—whispered of safety, of knowing one's place, of accepting limitations. However, I was discovering that transformation conveys a distinct language. It speaks of patience, of painful transformation, and of tiny victories intertwined like pearls on a string. Each scale practiced, each note held, each small step forward was another thread in the weaving of my wings.

Despite my frequent isolation during this transformation, a profound sense of confidence had become ingrained in me—a profound understanding, an unwavering conviction that the moment had arrived. The cocoon that had once protected me now felt like a prison. The air around me hummed with possibility, and my soul recognized its moment of emergence. All that remained was to trust in the wings I'd built in darkness.

Perhaps it's the remnant of that trapped caterpillar within me, but tell me something's impossible and you've lit the fuse of my determination. The audition day loomed, my heart pounding in my chest as I made my way to the music room. My hands trembled as I gripped the sheet music—a butterfly's first wingbeats, uncertain but necessary. Each step down that hallway felt like walking through deep water, weighted with fear yet buoyed by defiance.

The moment I opened my mouth to sing, something shifted in the universe. The notes that emerged were more than music—they were declarations of independence, proof of possibility. When the director

## THE BOY FROM BRAZIL                    65

smiled and welcomed me to the choir, I felt the first real weight drop into my bag of poker chips, solid and undeniable as gold. For the first time, I held something that was purely mine, earned through courage rather than compliance. That one "yes" served as the cornerstone of my new identity, marking the initial step towards my future self. Looking back now, I can trace the entire arc of my life to that moment of brave becoming—the day I finally learned to trust my wings.

In the harmonies of the choir, I discovered more than music—I found my tribe. After years of knowing only the carefully curated fellowship of church youth groups, where everyone wore the same spiritual uniform and spoke the same theological language, I suddenly found myself among people who celebrated diversity of expression. Each voice in the choir was unique, yet together we created something greater than ourselves. Each new friendship contributes to my increasing sense of self-worth, and every shared laugh and inside joke represents a small victory against isolation.

Our journeys through New Jersey transformed into journeys of exploration, with every show offering a fresh insight. The state theater revealed a world where art was crafted from shadow and light, bringing stories to life through the alchemy of design and dedication. I drank in everything—the technical magic of lighting, the architectural poetry of set design, the transformative power of makeup. In workshops and rehearsals, I found myself surrounded by people who didn't just dream but worked tirelessly to turn those dreams into reality. Here was a sanctuary built not of doctrine and prohibition but of creativity and possibility.

While my roots continued to search for stability, I sensed the initial stirrings of my authentic identity beginning to take root. News of "Alice in Wonderland" auditions captivated me, leading me into a world where I had to choose between obedience and growth. For the first time in my life, I faced my mother not as her miracle child but as a person becoming whole.

The confrontation crystallized our paradox: her love, forged in the crucible of my infant illness, had calcified into a cage of protection. Every "no" she spoke came from a place of profound fear—fear of losing me to the world, fear of failing God, fear of her own past coming back to claim her converted soul. I saw in her eyes the battle between the mother who had bargained with God for my life and the woman who had once danced with spirits in Brazil.

By God's grace, I've come to understand and forgive the fear that shaped her choices. But in that moment, I had to choose my own path. When I won not one but three roles in the play, the victory was bittersweet—each character I would portray felt like another small rebellion against her love. Yet something miraculous happened on opening night: my mother, sitting in the audience, witnessed not the death of her protection but the birth of something new. As she watched me transform on stage, I saw her own transformation begin—pride and fear dancing together in her eyes, just as they had in my heart.

## The Theater Kid

Raw talent, like an uncut diamond, sparkled within me—but the jagged edges of language still caught and snagged on my tongue. Rather than accept this limitation, I threw myself into a self-imposed apprenticeship of American theater. I devoured plays as if they were sacred texts, turning Thornton Wilder's words into my psalms and Neil Simon's dialogue into my daily sustenance. Each playwright offered a different flavor of American English, a new way of bending language to create truth on stage.

# THE BOY FROM BRAZIL

Every time our school announced productions such as "Our Town," "The Wiz," and "The Music Man," I would feel a surge of familiarity, akin to discovering old friends in a crowd. However, my sister's familiar cautionary words, "These roles are reserved for future theater majors," accompanied each audition notice. Don't set yourself up for disappointment... I just don't want to see you hurt." She meant well, but her warnings only fueled my determination.

I remembered my first time in the school theater as a middle schooler, neck craned back to study the constellation of stars that lined the walls—not celestial bodies, but golden emblems bearing the names of past performers. In that moment, something crystallized within me: a vision of my own name among those stars, not as a dream but as a prophecy. While others saw those stars as markers of past glory, I saw them as beacons lighting my path forward. My name belonged there; it was just a matter of time.

My teachers and I finally made a discovery that significantly improved my learning ability. No one had realized that being from Brazil, I always thought first in Portuguese. Whenever I had a lesson, I translated it in my mind to Portuguese and then to English, slowing me down to half the processing speed of everyone else. Overcoming this was huge for my progress and my confidence. As I started securing lead roles in the plays, my confidence skyrocketed. Eventually, just as I'd hoped, my name was finally on one of those stars! I can't accurately describe the feeling of accomplishment and pride this gave me. If life could have stopped there, I'd have been on the mountaintop forever. But life goes on.

Then came the breakthrough that would change everything—a moment of clarity as sudden and illuminating as stage lights snapping on. My teachers and I discovered the invisible wall I'd been climbing: my mind was still thinking in Portuguese, transforming every English word into my native tongue and back again, like a perpetual game of linguistic ping-pong. Each thought had to make two journeys before reaching my lips, leaving me perpetually running to catch up with my own mind.

Understanding the problem became the key to solving it. As I learned to think directly in English, it was like removing weights I hadn't known I was carrying. My mind, finally freed from its constant translation, soared. Lead roles that had seemed as distant as those golden stars began falling into my lap like ripe fruit. My bag of poker chips, once so light I feared a breath might scatter them, now grew heavy with the currency of success.

And then it happened—the day I stood beneath the theater wall, watching as my name was added to that constellation of performers. The golden star caught the light, throwing back a reflection that seemed to contain all my struggles and triumphs, all the prayers and tears and determination that had led to this moment. If I could have frozen time, captured that perfect crystal of achievement, and lived within it forever, I would have. But life, like theater, is all about movement—the next scene always waiting in the wings.

## Approaching Adulthood

Graduation day dawned bright with possibility, my diploma a passport to a future I could almost taste. My bag of poker chips, now heavy with theatrical triumph, clinked with each confident step toward community college. The stage had become more than my refuge—it was my identity, my truth, my answer to every question of who I was meant to be. In my dreams, I could already see my name in lights, stretching from Broadway to Hollywood in a constellation far grander than any high school wall could hold.

## THE BOY FROM BRAZIL                    69

The universe seemed to confirm my path when I landed a role in "Enter Laughing"—a play whose title felt like a cosmic wink at my journey from silence to center stage. But my parents' acceptance of my theatrical pursuits proved as ephemeral as stage makeup. Their old fears, barely buried beneath a thin layer of pride in my high school successes, resurfaced with renewed urgency. "Business school," they insisted, their voices heavy with practical concern. "Something stable, something secure." Their words carried echoes of their own transformation—from free spirits to fearful converts—and I recognized in their pleading the same desperate love that had once bargained with God for my life.

Freedom from my parents' fundamentalist fortress should have felt like liberation. Instead, it left me feeling as if I was in a state of constant limbo. The "real world" lacked the meticulously crafted scenes of high school theater, with no targets to meet, scripts to adhere to, and no assurance of applause at the conclusion of each performance. My carefully accumulated poker chips began slipping through my fingers like sand, each small setback stealing another piece of my hard-won confidence.

The social landscape shifted beneath my feet as friends scattered to distant universities, their departures leaving holes in my world that no amount of stage business could fill. Loneliness crept in like fog on an empty stage, making even familiar spaces feel strange and uncertain. The bright future I had envisioned, where talent and determination would lead me straight to success, started to blur and fade like old stage lights. My dream of a theater career, once so vivid I could taste it, now seemed to recede with each step I took toward it, like a mirage in the desert of adult reality.

Desperate to keep my theatrical dreams from dissolving completely, I invested what little money I had in Manhattan voice lessons and cabaret performances. Each subway ride into the city felt like a bridge between two worlds: the practical reality I was leaving behind and the glittering promise of what could be. But dreams, I was learning, had price tags. As my bank account dwindled and my debts mounted, I made the bitter choice to trade my college textbooks for real estate licenses, hoping that selling other people's dreams of home would somehow fund my own dreams of the stage.

I chased auditions like a desperate gambler chasing losses, but my old nemesis—language—had found me again. Cold readings became exercises in humiliation as my mind raced to process English faster than my Brazilian brain could manage. "Not authentic enough," the directors would say, their words cutting deeper than any script's dialogue. It's a peculiar paradox of theater that few outside the craft understand: the most convincing lies on stage come from the deepest truths within. To inhabit another character authentically, you must first know who you are. But my identity was as fragmented as my language skills—a collection of borrowed gestures and memorized emotions, with no solid core to ground them. The bitter irony lurking in the background was that I needed to discover my true self off stage before I could truly exist on it—a revelation that was still awaiting its cue.

The memory is carved in perfect detail: my cherry red Mustang, a theatrical prop in its own right, parked beneath the indifferent glare of a streetlamp after another failed audition. Inside, I was coming apart like a poorly constructed costume, my sobs the only audience to this unscripted performance. The stage had served as my guiding light, a constant in a life that was constantly changing. However, now that star had faded away, its light no longer able to guide me onward. All those golden stars from high school seemed to mock me now—fool's gold that had led me down a path of glittering disappointment.

THE BOY FROM BRAZIL                           71

The cruel truth was settling in like dust after the final curtain: talent
and determination weren't always enough. We all secretly believe we'll
be the exception, the one whose name breaks through in lights, whose
story becomes legend. I had believed it with the fierce certainty of
youth and had never imagined my journey would include these scenes
of defeat. But here I sat, in a car the color of passion and warning signs,
learning that sometimes the most important roles we play are in the
scenes we never wanted to rehearse.

## Finding Myself Through Relationships

The occasional role still came my way, but each performance felt increasingly hollow, like reading lines in an empty theater. My precious
poker chips—once gleaming with promise—were now tarnished to-
kens in a game I was losing. Depression crept in like a shadow seeping
under a stage door, darkening even my brightest moments. In this
twilight of identity, I began searching for new spotlights to stand in,
new mirrors to reflect back some version of myself I could recognize.

Relationships beckoned like method acting exercises—a chance to
become someone new through the eyes of another. Perhaps, I thought,
I could find my character through romantic connection, could understand my role in the world through someone else's script. I began
collecting potential co-stars, hoping their desire could substitute for
my own self-knowledge, that their passion could fill the void where
my identity should have been.

The faith of my childhood watched from the wings, its judgmental
gaze heavy on my shoulders. But what authority did it have now?
That religion had been nothing but a cramped dressing room, its
mirrors showing only approved reflections, its costume rack offering
only pre-approved roles. At least in these new relationships, I thought,

I could try on different versions of myself and could experiment with who I might become.

As relationships with women failed to fill the emptiness, my desperate search for authenticity led me down unexpected paths. Maybe, I reasoned, my true self lay in a different direction entirely. The possibility of same-sex attraction emerged like a controversial plot twist—terrifying yet somehow compelling. Here was another stage to perform on, another identity to try on. But what I thought might be self-discovery was really self-destruction in disguise. In this vulnerable state, my fears became an open invitation to darker influences. The enemy, ever the opportunist, saw his chance to rewrite my story entirely, to turn my identity crisis into his victory.

The revelation would come later, like a spotlight slowly rising on an empty stage: Jesus was the ultimate model of unshakeable identity. When Satan tempted Him in the wilderness—that cosmic audition where the enemy attempted to make Him doubt His role—Jesus remained steadfast for one transcendent reason: He knew, with unwavering certainty, that He was God's beloved Son. This wasn't just a line He'd memorized; it was the core truth of His being.

How different this was from the fundamentalist theater of fear where I'd grown up, where God was portrayed as more director than father, more critic than lover. The script I'd been handed contained all His demands but none of His devotion, all His standards but none of His tenderness. Those endless Sunday night sermons were like watching the same dark tragedy again and again—all thunder and judgment, no grace or redemption. God's love, if mentioned at all, felt like a prop rather than the central theme.

So when my soul echoed with emptiness—that God-shaped void that no amount of applause could fill—I never thought to look toward heaven. The God I knew was all closed curtains and locked doors, all rules and regulations. Why would I run to Him? Yes, I was the prodigal son, but I had never experienced the father's embrace before. The path home seemed not just distant but nonexistent, obscured by years of religious smoke and mirrors. What reason did I have to believe that anything awaited me there but more judgment, more performance reviews, and more failed auditions for an impossible role?

## Towards My New Identity in Christ

A soul without identity in Christ is like an actor without a script, improvising desperately on an endless stage. Only when we discover who we are in Him does the world transform from a threatening arena into an open playground of possibility. But this discovery requires space—sacred space to explore, to question, to stumble, and to soar.

Looking back at my theatrical rebellion through the lens of grace, I see now how far behind I truly was. While my peers had been given permission to try on different roles in life's great performance, I remained trapped in my religious cocoon, watching their wings unfold through the silken walls of my confinement. My journey began not just in a foreign country, but in a foreign understanding of God—one that emphasized containment over growth, protection over exploration.

The greatest gift a parent can offer their child isn't perfect safety but sacred freedom—the freedom to make mistakes within the safety net of unconditional love. Yes, watching your child stumble is like watching an actor forget their lines on opening night—heart-stopping, painful, terrifying. But without these moments of beautiful imperfection, how can any of us learn our true role in God's grand production?

Dreams and visions are the spotlight that illuminates our path forward. Without them, we become extras in our own life story, shuffling through scenes without purpose or direction. Helen Keller's wisdom, "The only thing worse than being blind is having sight but no vision," resonates timeless. Coming from one who lived in physical darkness, these words cast a powerful light on the difference between merely seeing life's stage and truly envisioning our role upon it.

Dreams and visions are like divine stage directions, guiding us toward the role we were born to play. Each of us carries within us a unique purpose—a solo performance waiting to be discovered. Our deepest longings often point like spotlights toward our hidden talents, illuminating the intersection where passion meets ability. This sacred convergence of gifts and calling is where we find our truest purpose, where our personal script aligns perfectly with the Great Director's vision

Consider Michael Jordan's story—not just a tale of athletic prowess, but a masterclass in divine persistence. When the sophomore basketball team rejected him due to his short stature, it could have marked the end of his career. Instead, it became merely an early-act setback in what would become a legendary performance. Six NBA championships and three MVP awards later, his story stands as a testament to what happens when we refuse to let early rejections write our ending. Jordan discovered his unique fusion of divinely inspired dreams and divinely gifted abilities, resulting in a unique blend that surpasses mere athletic accomplishments and embodies living poetry.

Every God-given dream faces its own wilderness journey, its own series of trials and temptations. The path to purpose often winds through valleys of doubt and mountains of opposition. But when a vision bears the watermark of divine origin, it carries within it the seeds of its own fulfillment. Like a play written in heaven, the ending is

# THE BOY FROM BRAZIL

already secured—though the middle acts may test every ounce of our faith and perseverance.

Consider Joseph, who epitomizes the concept of delayed gratification. His story reads like an epic drama: the dreamer son of Jacob, whose visions of future glory earned him both a multicolored coat and his brothers' murderous envy. From favored son to slave, from trusted servant to falsely accused prisoner, Joseph's journey seemed to lead everywhere except toward the fulfillment of his dreams. For seventeen years, he lived in the tension between divine promise and earthly reality. Imagine if he had abandoned hope in year fifteen, not knowing that his greatest scene—his transformation from prisoner to prince—was merely two years away. His story reminds us that God's timing has its own perfect rhythm, and what looks like a lengthy intermission may actually be crucial character development in heaven's playbill.

Dream boldly, not only for your own life, but for an enduring acclaim. Extend your visions beyond your own comprehension, as it's within the immensity of unattainable dreams that we uncover our profound yearning for the Ultimate Director. When we dare to dream beyond our human capabilities, we find ourselves drawn inexorably toward the One who holds all futures in His hands, the Master Storyteller who has already written the final act of history.

Each day becomes a rehearsal for eternity when we approach it with both heavenly vision and earthly wisdom. Balance your dreaming with doing, your soaring with stepping. And don't journey alone—find fellow players in God's grand production who can support your role and celebrate your victories. For in the end, we're all part of an ensemble cast in the greatest story ever told, each playing our unique part in God's magnificent performance of redemption.

## Points for Reflection

1. Think back to your childhood dreams—what did you want to be when you grew up? How have your goals or aspirations changed over time, and what influenced those changes?

2. How do you feel about your current career or life path? Are you finding joy and purpose in it, and if not, what might be missing or holding you back?

3. Imagine pursuing your dreams without grounding them in your identity in Christ. How might that affect your values, decisions, and sense of purpose? How does keeping Christ at the center transform the way you approach your goals and ambitions?

# Chapter 5

# The Fall

*"And the Lord's servant must not be quarrelsome but kind to everyone, able to teach, patiently enduring evil, correcting his opponents with gentleness. God may perhaps grant them repentance leading to a knowledge of the truth, and they may come to their senses and escape from the snare of the devil after being captured by him to do his will."*
*2 Timothy 2:24-26*

*"Resentment is like drinking poison and then hoping it will kill your enemies."*
*- Nelson Mandela*

### Anointed Warrior

Beneath the shepherd's cloth, a warrior sleeps
Through palace halls, they hunted royalty
His brothers stood tall, crowned by mortal glory
Yet heaven's gaze fell elsewhere, defying reason
In valleys deep, he walked his solitary path

Through wilderness of stone and shadow-thought
Dark waters rose to drown his fractured faith
Each demon met its match in midnight hours
In fields where darkness blooms, he wielded light
His spirit, torn and scattered to the winds,
Haunted by whispers of unworthiness—
These shadows that devoured his peace
He bore their judgment like a crown of thorns
His palms still burning with divine purpose
The world, a chorus of contempt,
Called him from his quiet battles,
Their laughter sharp as broken glass,
Their whispers poison-tipped,
Their scorn a weight to bear
Then sacred oil anointed destiny
They never glimpsed the lion in his heart,
Never knew the strength beneath his scars,
Never witnessed glory in his depths
For he had slain his giants long before
With faith sharper than any blade
He rose above their doubt...and conquered

## Guerreiro Ungido

Sob as vestes do pastor, um guerreiro dorme
Pelos salões do palácio, buscavam realeza
Seus irmãos erguiam-se altivos, coroados de glória mortal
Mas o olhar divino pousou alhures, desafiando a razão
Em vales profundos, trilhou seu caminho solitário

## THE BOY FROM BRAZIL

Por desertos de pedra e pensamentos sombrios
Águas escuras ergueram-se para afogar sua fé fragmentada
Cada demônio encontrou seu igual nas horas da meia-noite
Em campos onde a escuridão floresce, ele empunhou a luz
Seu espírito, dilacerado e espalhado aos ventos,
Assombrado por sussurros de indignidade—
Essas sombras que devoravam sua paz
Suportou seus julgamentos como uma coroa de espinhos
Suas palmas ainda ardendo com propósito divino
O mundo, um coro de desprezo,
Chamou-o de suas batalhas silenciosas,
Suas risadas afiadas como vidro quebrado,
Seus sussurros envenenados,
Seu escárnio um fardo a carregar
Então o óleo sagrado ungiu o destino
Nunca vislumbraram o leão em seu coração,
Nunca conheceram a força sob suas cicatrizes,
Nunca testemunharam a glória em suas profundezas
Pois ele já havia matado seus gigantes muito antes
Com fé mais afiada que qualquer lâmina
Ele se ergueu acima da dúvida...e conquistou

The world shimmered with endless temptations, each more se-ductive than the last. I found myself trapped in a gilded cage of my own making, its bars forged from desires I couldn't name. Before I could even think to search for an escape—before I understood there might be a key—the walls began their slow, inexorable advance. My anguish, once a quiet whisper, grew into a deafening roar as I burned beneath the merciless sun of my own desires.

Lust became my first stumble down a path that would lead me far from grace, each step echoing with consequences I couldn't yet comprehend.

It simmered beneath my skin like molten metal, this force I couldn't control. Whether I was sequestered in my bedroom's false sanctuary or wandering the twilight streets like a lost soul, lust weakened my knees and clouded my mind. When it reached its fever pitch, my legs would tremble like autumn leaves in a storm. My skin would flush crimson, not with illness but with something far more insidious. There were no physical symptoms to identify and no medication to alleviate my condition. Instead, I was struck with a different kind of blindness—one that didn't darken the world but rather painted it in false colors.

Lust prevented me from seeing the world through the same eyes I was used to. Soon, colors became so bright that I could hardly distinguish them from each other. It felt as if I was staring at the sun, spots clouding my vision, something else taking over from me and moving my body this way and that way. I experienced a complete loss of control.

Like a ship lost in stormy seas, I gradually realized the worldly lifestyle was steering me toward destruction. An anchor of guilt weighed on my soul, threatening to drag me into the depths. Yet my understanding then was as fragmented as a broken mirror—I could only see pieces of the truth, distorted and incomplete. Something vital was missing from my life, a void as vast as the ocean itself, though I couldn't name what would fill it. Amid the tempest of these overwhelming feelings, I began to dive deeper, each question I asked myself leading to another, like following a chain into darker waters.

Who was the person beneath this carefully crafted facade? What lay behind the mask I showed the world? Which star should guide

# THE BOY FROM BRAZIL

my wayward ship? What treasures did I truly cherish deep within my heart?

Yet even as I posed these profound questions, my answers remained as shallow as tide pools. Each reflective surface became a trap—store windows, phone screens, mirrors—all conspiring to hold me captive to my own image. My reflection morphed into an idol, a false god I worshipped with religious devotion. I honed my appearance like a weapon, believing that if I could just perfect this outer shell, I could pierce through others' defenses and find the connection I so desperately craved.

What drove this relentless pursuit of perfection? The answer pulsed through my veins like poison—lust had become not just my motivation, but my very reason for existing. I think now of a butterfly emerging from its chrysalis, wings still damp with transformation. How fortunate it is, never having to confront its own reflection, never becoming ensnared by its own beauty. Nature, in her wisdom, spares the butterfly this burden of self-awareness. Yet paradoxically, my descent into the depths of lust and self-absorption became the crucible that would eventually forge my understanding of true humanity. Like that metamorphosing butterfly, I had to pass through darkness to find my wings.

The perils of unbridled desire lurk like quicksand beneath seemingly solid ground, waiting to claim any unwary soul who ventures too close. Only now, looking back through time's clarifying lens, can I fully grasp the magnitude of my misguided path. Each surrender to lust was another brick in a wall between myself and God, a barrier built by my own hands. My unregenerate heart had twisted the very concept of need, mistaking hunger for nourishment and thirst for water. I chased the mirage of romantic love, desperate for validation, addicted to the hollow echo of others' admiration. These false idols I called "needs" became my religion, and I prostrated myself before them until they nearly consumed me whole.

## Who Am I Really?

My mother, a missionary whose life testified to deeper truths, had tried to plant seeds of faith in my young heart. But those seeds fell on rocky soil—my childhood self found no sustenance in religion's ancient wisdom. As soon as I stepped off the plane in America, the allure of mainstream culture captivated me, compelling me to abandon my outsider status. Like a moth drawn to artificial light, I followed my peers into their world of carefully curated appearances, soap-opera relationships, and gleaming superficiality. Their hollow gospel of self-image became my new scripture.

The question "Why?" haunted me like a persistent shadow. How could something as ephemeral as physical beauty, as fleeting as others' approval, hold such tyrannical power over my soul? What made me willing to lay my authentic self upon this altar of appearances, sacrificing everything genuine for a handful of hollow praise? Hindsight illuminates these questions with painful clarity, but back then, I was too entangled in the web of my own making to see the spider that waited at its center.

In desperate moments, I would send whispered prayers into the darkness, begging God to part the veil of confusion that shrouded my heart. Even as lust's tide continued to pull me under, something deep within yearned for understanding, for transformation. At thirteen, the ground beneath my feet began to shift—my carefully constructed self-image cracked like a mirror struck by lightning. My identity unraveled like water, compelling me to embark on a journey of self-exploration. Like a butterfly testing new wings, I ventured far beyond

# THE BOY FROM BRAZIL

the familiar garden of my comfort zone, seeking wisdom in strange and distant blooms.

Though I explore this journey more deeply elsewhere, this truth rings like a crystal bell through all my chapters: God bestows upon us a single, sacred identity. We are His children, crafted with divine intention, bearing His image like precious gems reflect light. Any lesser identity—any counterfeit self we try to fashion—becomes a hollow shell that echoes with emptiness, a maze where we lose ourselves in endless confusion.

As I stumbled through the labyrinth of self-discovery, twin demons of lust and anger became my toxic guides, leading me deeper into darkness with each misguided step. For years, I remained blind to the connection between the tempest in my heart and the destruction in my wake. As chaos consumed my world like a spreading wildfire, I fled further into the night, desperately seeking escape in the very things that burned me. I tried to drown my pain in an ocean of bad habits, each new vice promising relief but delivering only deeper wounds. Before I could confront the harsh reality, I mastered the art of evading my own shadow, oblivious to the fact that it would trail me wherever I ventured.

## Mirror, Mirror on the Wall, Am I the Fairest of Them All?

Manhattan's glittering skyline haunted my dreams like a mirage in the desert, promising an oasis of endless possibility. Each morning, I'd stand before my mirror like a devotee at an altar, whispering to my reflection, "With this face, the world will bow at your feet." My beauty became my currency, my youth a finite investment that I desperately needed to invest in before it faded away. I convinced myself that maintaining this perfect exterior would somehow fill the growing void within—a chasm that deepened with each passing day. The prophet Jeremiah's words now strike me with devastating clarity: "For my people have committed two evils: they have forsaken me, the fountain of living waters, and hewed out cisterns for themselves, broken cisterns that can hold no water." I had become an architect of empty vessels, crafting elaborate containers that could never hold the living water my soul truly craved.

Though I hadn't actively forsaken God—how could I forsake someone I'd never truly known?—I had become a master craftsman of broken cisterns, each more elaborate than the last. Like the people of Jeremiah's time, like countless souls today, I was dying of thirst while chasing mirages, drinking salt water to quench a thirst that only pure springs could satisfy. Each false solution left me more parched, more hollow, and more desperate for the next illusory promise of fulfillment

My life became an endless carousel of neon nights and artificial dawns—Friday's party bled into Saturday's revelry, which spilled into Sunday's recovery, only to begin again. Like a moth drawn to destructive flames, I chased the next gathering, the next crowd, the next chance to lose myself in the pulsing rhythm of escape. I fluttered from one glittering scene to another, a dark parody of the butterfly seeking nectar—but where the butterfly finds sustenance, I found only emptiness dressed in sequins and strobe lights. The hollowness of it all never registered; I was too intoxicated by my own perceived invincibility, too caught up in the delusion that youth and beauty made me untouchable. My mother's missionary work, once a steady lighthouse beam in my childhood, faded to a distant pinprick of light on a horizon I no longer cared to seek. Her sacred purpose became nothing more than a fading photograph in the scrapbook of a life I was determined to leave behind.

## THE BOY FROM BRAZIL

During those glitzy moments, I genuinely thought I had everything valuable. Such is the cunning nature of temptation—it wraps itself in beautiful lies, making the poison taste like honey. We've all drunk from this deceptive cup in our own ways, mistaking spiritual malnourishment for fulfillment. The Bible speaks of a "seared conscience" (1 Timothy 4:2), and mine had been cauterized by the hot iron of desire, rendered numb to the very pain that might have saved me

As masters of self-deception, we humans slowly sink into quicksand, deceiving ourselves into believing we are learning to float. Like a tree being hollowed out by invisible termites, we often don't recognize the destruction until we're on the verge of collapse. I wore my shame like an invisible cloak, its weight increasing day by day until I was bent double—yet still I denied its existence. The truth screamed at me through sleepless nights and tear-stained mornings, but I had become fluent in the language of denial, translating every warning sign into another excuse to push forward.

Yet beneath my carefully constructed facade, a void yawned wider with each passing day.

Faith, the crucial link between the visible and invisible, had long since vanished from my life. Even when reality tried to shake me awake with brutal metaphors—like the day my apartment erupted in flames, devoured by fire sparked by a contractor's careless work—I remained stubbornly blind. The devastation of my haven, the sole refuge in a turbulent life, ought to have served as a stark reminder. Instead, I painted over the ashes with fresh delusions, plastering new wallpaper over charred walls. The inferno that consumed my physical shelter merely foreshadowed the spiritual conflagration consuming my soul, yet I remained committed to my path of destruction, convinced that the smoke in my lungs was actually sweet perfume.

I remained trapped in my spiral of self-destruction even when trust shattered like glass against concrete—when someone I'd given my heart to repaid that gift with both visible and hidden bruises. The physical and emotional abuse should have served as a stark warning, but I had become too adept at ignoring reality. Instead of turning toward faith's healing light, I stumbled through a hall of mirrors, desperately seeking completion in the reflections of others. I handed out pieces of myself like party favors to everyone I met, naively believing they would return these fragments made whole. But they were spiritual vampires, taking what they needed and leaving me more hollow than before, their own emptiness echoing my own.

At the core of this self-destructive dance lay a garden of insecurities, their roots reaching deep into the parched soil of my soul. I was a vessel made of smoke, dissipating at the slightest touch, unable to hold onto my own truth or stand against the winds of wrong. Each dawn brought a fresh round of self-deception as I whispered sweet poison into my own ear: "The pain is temporary. The right person will heal everything." I placed all my hopes in this mythical savior, envisioning them as a radiant butterfly that would land on my withered flower and transform it into an eternal bloom. Oh, the bitter irony—for my true Savior had been waiting all along, patient as eternity, while I chased paper butterflies through storms of my own making.

## Dancing with Delusion: When Truth Becomes Fluid

Beyond the thorny garden of my insecurities sprawled a wasteland of misconceptions, where truth itself had become as malleable as clay in my hands. Like a mathematician convinced that two plus two could equal whatever I needed it to be, I had constructed an entire universe of comfortable lies. The stark reality of good and evil—as fundamental

# THE BOY FROM BRAZIL

as gravity, as unchangeable as the North Star—had dissolved into a fog of moral relativism. When confronted with darkness, I would adjust my vision rather than acknowledge the shadows. If someone's actions sent warning signals flaring through my consciousness, I would dim my own inner light until their darkness seemed normal, even beautiful.

This fluid morality was my misguided attempt to embrace the often-quoted words of Jesus: 'Judge not lest you be judged' (Matthew 7:1). But in my desperate attempt to avoid judgment, I had twisted this divine wisdom into something unrecognizable and deeply destructive. Like a compass whose needle has been magnetized by lightning, I had lost my ability to distinguish true north from south. This wasn't the discernment Jesus called for—it was spiritual blindness masquerading as enlightenment.

Paul's words in Romans thunder across the centuries with devastating precision: *"Therefore you have no excuse, O man, every one of you who judges. For in passing judgment on another, you condemn yourself because you, the judge, practice the very same things... Do you suppose, O man—you who judge those who practice such things and yet do them yourself—that you will escape the judgment of God?"* (Romans 2:1-3). These verses illuminated the landscape of my own hypocrisy in stark relief, striking me like lightning striking a midnight sky.

The heart of the matter wasn't about abstaining from all judgment—it was about the poisonous paradox of condemning in others what we embrace in ourselves. Like a performer in a Greek tragedy wearing a mask of righteousness while acting out the very sins they denounce, I had become skilled in the art of selective blindness. The true path forward wasn't to abandon all moral distinction but to first turn that penetrating light inward, to excavate the darkness in our own hearts before presuming to illuminate the shadows in others.

This moral contradiction had etched deep chasms of insecurity into my psyche. When we christen darkness as light, when we perfume decay and call it fragrance, we splinter our own souls. Deep in the marrow of our being, we recognize the lie—and this knowledge corrodes our self-trust like acid eating through metal. Every time we submerge evil into the realm of rationalization, we progressively weaken our internal compass, ultimately leading us to lose trust in even our own sense of direction.

Such spiritual double vision fractures the very foundation of self-worth. Even when we grasp the transformative truth that God accepts us—that He writes our true identity in eternal ink—we cannot fully embrace this gift while living in a house built of lies. No amount of divine love can stabilize a soul that insists on calling darkness light, just as no mathematical system can function if we insist that two plus two equals three. When we step into God's light, we must let it illuminate everything, even the shadows we've grown comfortable hiding within. Truth isn't just a concept—it's the oxygen our spirits need to breathe.

The devil is not merely a metaphor or a primitive explanation for human wickedness—he exists with the same certainty as the air we breathe. Back when I was lost in the funhouse mirrors of self-absorption, dreaming of Manhattan's glittering promises, such a notion seemed as outdated as my mother's missionary work. In those days, when I couldn't pass a reflective surface without stopping to admire my own image, when every daydream starred me conquering New York like some modern-day Helen of Troy, the idea of a literal devil felt like a joke from a less enlightened age. My mother's faith, her warnings about spiritual warfare, bounced off the armor of my presumed sophistication like pebbles off plate glass. The devil's greatest triumph,

# THE BOY FROM BRAZIL

I would later learn, was convincing me he was nothing more than a punchline.

## Night Terrors and Dark Revelations

My carefully constructed world of self-delusion shattered, not in the harsh light of day, but in the vulnerable darkness of my dreams. Like a house of cards collapsing in slow motion, my reality began to crumble in those unguarded hours when consciousness slips its moorings and truth speaks in shadows.

In my arrogance, I had challenged God to prove the existence of darkness, as if evil were a scientific theorem awaiting verification. "Show me," I had demanded, like a child daring the monster under the bed to reveal itself. At thirteen, my challenge was answered—not with gentle persuasion, but with a series of nightmarish visions that would brand themselves into my psyche like hot iron on flesh. Be careful what you pray for, they say. God, in His terrible mercy, was about to give me exactly what I had asked for.

Oh, I knew evil existed in the world's daylight hours—it screamed from headlines about child trafficking, whispered through the echoes of continued slavery, painted itself in the stark colors of racism and hatred. But these horrors, as real as they were, could be rationalized away by those who preferred their demons dressed in psychological theories and sociological explanations. In my sophisticated ignorance, I had joined the chorus of modern voices that explained away even the most horrific acts as mere products of circumstance—"He was abused, so he became an abuser." We had become masters of excusing the inexcusable, of finding clinical terms for what was, at its core, pure evil. I wanted proof beyond these comfortable explanations, beyond the reach of rational interpretation. And in the darkness of my dreams, that proof came hunting for me.

The first visitation came in the form of a dark pursuer—a figure carved from midnight itself, with hair like liquid darkness flowing past his shoulders. In this recurring nightmare, my feet would pound against endless corridors, my lungs burning with exhaustion, but no amount of running could put distance between us. The space between us seemed to fold like a cosmic origami, bringing him ever closer despite my desperate flight. Three times this shadow hunter stalked through my dreams, and each visitation left deep wounds in my waking life—waves of depression that crashed over me like black tide, anxiety that wrapped around my throat like spectral fingers

Then came the dream that turned my sanctuary into a trap. In the false safety of my own bed, a hand would materialize from the darkness beneath—not the clumsy grab of a childhood monster, but the deliberate reach of ancient malevolence. My attempts to fight back were like trying to punch smoke; my desperate swats met with flesh that felt like cold iron. That grotesque limb would lock around me with the inexorable grip of a serpent, dragging me toward the void beneath my bed. I would thrash and struggle, my screams trapped in my throat, but my strength was nothing against this force that seemed to draw power from the darkness itself.

These nocturnal terrors deeply penetrated my psyche, gradually weakening my mental defenses as if they were a form of torture. The moments after each nightmare became their own kind of hell—I would lie rigid in my bed, eyes wide and burning, too terrified to risk falling back into sleep's treacherous embrace. Night after night, I kept my vigil until dawn, watching shadows dance on my walls like mocking spectators. The butterflies and roses of normal life became distant memories, impossible to appreciate through the fog of exhaustion and the constant, gnawing fear that something waited in the darkness, patient and hungry, for me to lower my guard

The third nightmare brought a different kind of horror—a chorus of shadow-wreathed figures that encircled my bed like dark sentinels at a perverted vigil. These entities didn't need physical violence; their weapons were words that cut deeper than any blade. Their voices dripped with ancient venom, each syllable precisely crafted to pierce my deepest insecurities. Despite my attempts to shield myself with my body, their sharp accusations penetrated every weakness in my defenses. The psychological torture was so intense that I found myself longing for the relative mercy of the grabbing arm beneath my bed—a chilling revelation of how we humans often flee from one torment to another, trading one demon's embrace for another's chains. Like addicts switching poisons, we dance from gluttony to vanity, from lust to pride, each new sin promising escape from the last, each one tightening its own unique noose around our souls.

But the most terrifying visitations were reserved for nights spent away from home, as if these entities delighted in catching me at my most vulnerable. In the unfamiliar darkness of a friend's house, demons would materialize—not the cartoonish creatures of Hollywood imagination, but beings of such ancient malevolence that their mere presence made reality feel thin and brittle. They would lean close, their whispered questions burrowing into my mind like parasitic worms, their voices building from seductive murmurs to soul-shattering screams. These interrogations felt like spiritual vivisection, each question peeling back another layer of my psyche until I lay exposed and helpless before their terrible scrutiny.

But the darkness wasn't content to remain confined to my dreams—it began seeping into my waking hours like ink bleeding through paper. Reality itself seemed to grow thin and permeable. Sitting at my desk in broad daylight, I would catch glimpses of shadows that moved with terrible purpose, their movements too deliberate to be tricks of the light. My familiar kitchen, once a place of comfort and sustenance, would transform before my eyes into a medieval dungeon, its walls weeping with ancient malice. Then, as if Hell itself were impatient to reveal its true face, the dungeon would dissolve into a nightmare landscape of flame and shadow—a vision of the inferno that made Dante's descriptions seem tame. I watched in helpless horror as demons performed their obscene ballet of consumption, each horror devouring another in an endless cycle of corruption, their bodies melding and separating in ways that defied both physics and sanity. The sight burned itself into my mind like a photographer's negative, impossible to unsee.

A moment of terrible clarity pierced through the madness amidst this infernal chaos. One demon—wearing the deceptively ordinary face of a man, like a wolf dressed in sheep's clothing—turned its gaze directly upon me. Our eyes met across the gulf between worlds, and its words fell into my mind like stones into a still pond:

"The chief is coming to pay you a visit," it announced with the casual malice of someone delivering a death sentence.

Terror exploded in my gut like molten lead as my eyes were drawn inexorably over the demon's shoulder. There, stretching across what had once been my kitchen wall, loomed a shadow that seemed to devour light itself—a towering figure crowned with horns that curved like scythes against the infernal glow. Its robes rippled like liquid darkness, each fold containing universes of shadow. When it moved, reality trembled. Each footfall sent shockwaves through the fabric of existence, as if the world itself recoiled from its touch. The vibrations threatened to either crack the earth open beneath my feet or launch

# THE BOY FROM BRAZIL

me into the void of space, leaving me to drift eternally through the cold darkness between stars.

In the presence of such primordial malevolence, I felt my very soul shrinking, trying to make itself invisible before this avatar of darkness. But the most horrifying revelation wasn't the demon's appearance—it was the sudden, crushing understanding that I had helped build its bridge into my world. Every act of lust, every moment of using others as objects for my pleasure, and every selfish manipulation had contributed to the path that led directly to my kitchen door. I had been my own betrayer, carving doorways between worlds with tools forged from my own sins. My pursuit of pleasure had become a beacon in the dark, drawing these entities not just into my home but into the very architecture of my mind.

Ephesians 4:25-27, "Therefore, having put away falsehood, let each one of you speak the truth with his neighbor, for we are members one of another," rang through my mind with terrifying clarity. Be angry and do not sin; do not let the sun go down on your anger, and give no opportunity to the devil."

Paul's warning wasn't just spiritual poetry—it was a battlefield manual for the soul. Some translations render it more starkly: "Don't give the devil a foothold." I now understood this metaphor in all its horrifying literalness. Like a mountain climber hammering pitons into sheer rock, I had been unknowingly driving anchors into my soul, creating handholds for darkness to climb. Every lie, every moment of unresolved anger, and every act of lust had been another invitation, another secure point for evil to grip and pull itself closer to my heart. I hadn't just given the devil a foothold—I had built him an entire climbing wall, and now he was reaching the summit of my soul. Through my choices, I had transformed into a house, leaving every door unlocked and every window wide open to the night, essentially inviting the darkness to settle in.

## The Twisted Dance of Love and Hate

The modern world had sculpted me with cruel hands, shaping me into a vessel of its own emptiness—a hollow chalice filled with nothing but echoing despair. Too eager to love and too quick to forgive, my heart became a magnet for those who would injure me. I scattered trust like seeds on barren ground, watching them wither and die in soil poisoned by betrayal. The Bible speaks of two eternal kingdoms locked in cosmic combat—the realm of light, where truth blazes like a thousand suns, and the kingdom of darkness, where shadows breed more shadows. I had unwittingly pledged my allegiance to the latter, building my house in the valley of shadows, decorating its walls with beautiful lies.

Small wonder, then, that my identity had become as insubstantial as morning mist—a shape-shifting specter that refused to solidify. The mirror became my daily battlefield, where I confronted a paradox: a face I worshipped and a soul I could barely recognize. How could I simultaneously adore and despise the person staring back at me? The answer lay in the perfect mask I had crafted—a gleaming facade that could charm the world while concealing the trembling, authentic self beneath. I had become my own greatest deception, constructing an elaborate hologram of beauty and confidence while the real me languished in the shadows, starved for light and truth.

With each passing night, the darkness grew denser, more tangible—a living thing that breathed and expanded until it infiltrated every corner of my existence. The demons no longer required an invitation; they had staked their claim to my soul. During the darkest moments, when hope appeared as far away as the stars above the storm clouds, I found myself engulfed by the repercussions of my own decisions, with each breath I took drawing me further into the depths of despair.

Yet even in this spiritual wasteland, pinpoints of light pierced the darkness—stories of redemption that had survived the centuries. There was Paul, once a breathing engine of persecution, his hands stained with Christians' blood, whom God transformed into His most passionate apostle. There was Peter, whose three denials of Christ rang out like death knells in the night, yet whose restoration became a testament to divine love's persistence. These stories should have been lifelines of hope.

But then there was Judas—the cautionary tale that haunted my thoughts. Here was a man so thoroughly inhabited by darkness that redemption seemed to recoil from him. Not because God's grace was insufficient, but because Judas himself had become a black hole of spirit, collapsing inward with such force that even light couldn't escape. His regret, bitter as wormwood, never blossomed into true repentance. In him, I saw my own reflection—a soul so saturated with Satan's influence that it had become a conductor for darkness.

Yet even this realization was, paradoxically, a mercy. Through these nightmarish visions, God was holding up a mirror to my soul, answering my demands for proof with terrible clarity. I had asked to see the darkness—now I was seeing it not just around me but within me, and the revelation was both devastating and necessary for any hope of redemption.

## Blind to the Divine Semaphore

Like a sailor ignoring storm clouds on the horizon, I willfully misread the warning signs God was painting across my nights. Instead of seeing these dreams as warning lights on my soul's dashboard, I questioned why I was the only one seemingly cursed with such torment. All around me, others appeared to float effortlessly through life, their smiles as bright as summer days, while I struggled through an endless twilight of my own making.

My eyes were fixed only on the surface of things—like someone admiring their reflection in a poisoned well. I had yet to grasp the profound truth that true beauty emanates from within, that external charm without internal grace is merely a painted sepulcher. Nature herself had been trying to teach me this lesson all along through her most exquisite messengers: butterflies.

These living stained-glass windows don't just wear their beauty like a costume—their entire existence is a testament to harmony between inner and outer splendor. Their delicate wings don't just carry them from flower to flower; they become instruments of life itself, spreading pollen like priests dispensing blessings, turning each garden into a cathedral of creation. They take only what they need and, in the process, give life to entire ecosystems. Their beauty isn't just aesthetic—it's functional, purposeful, and holy.

Looking back now, I see this is the sacred algorithm of a life well-lived: to become a channel of grace, to take only what sustains us while giving back more than we receive. However, achieving such transformation is not a simple task. Like the butterfly, I had to endure my time in the chrysalis—that dark night of the soul where old identities dissolve into primordial soup before new life can emerge. I measured my metamorphosis not in days but in years, with each moment of darkness creating another rip in the wings I would eventually spread.

# Fortresses of Darkness: Understanding Spiritual Strongholds

How does one wage war against an enemy they cannot see? This is the crucial question facing every soul trapped behind the walls of spiritual strongholds—those ancient fortresses of darkness that most people don't even realize exist. In the natural world, a stronghold is a fortress built for protection, a citadel designed to withstand siege. But in the spiritual realm, these structures become prisons masquerading as shelters, chains disguised as shields.

Think of these strongholds as generational architecture—dark castles built stone by stone through family histories, their foundations laid in trauma and reinforced by repeated sins. They pass down like toxic heirlooms: the tower of sexual immorality, the dungeon of depression, and the battlement of rage. Each generation adds its own rooms, its own shadows, until the fortress becomes a labyrinth of inherited bondage.

Living in ignorance of these strongholds is akin to fighting without a map, attempting to confront an invisible foe while keeping your feet bound to the territory you're attempting to seize. It's like trying to treat cancer with band-aids—you might cover the surface symptoms, but the real battle rages far deeper, in places only spiritual eyes can see.

Beyond the veil of physical reality rages an ancient war—a cosmic conflict that most of us glimpse only in shadows and echoes. This is spiritual warfare, not a metaphor or primitive superstition, but a war as real as any fought with steel and gunpowder, yet infinitely more consequential. Since Lucifer's first rebellion scattered stars across the heavens, this war has shaped the destiny of every human soul. The battlefield stretches across both seen and unseen realms, and the casualties are counted not in bodies but in souls.

Choosing Christ as your ally sets your spirit on fire. As Ephesians 6:12 reveals with chilling clarity, "For our struggle is not against flesh and blood, but against the rulers, against the authorities, against the powers of this dark world, and against the spiritual forces of evil in the heavenly realms." These aren't mere poetic flourishes—they're military intelligence reports from the front lines of a war that's been raging since before time began.

When we kneel before Christ, we essentially sign our enlistment papers in this cosmic conflict. Whether we whisper it or shout it, our allegiance to God automatically makes us adversaries of the Enemy. But here's the glorious truth: we're not sent into battle unequipped. God, the master strategist, has provided us with armor forged in heaven's own armory. As Paul writes in Ephesians 6:10-11, "Finally, be strong in the Lord and in His mighty power. Put on the full armor of God so that you can make your stand against the devil's schemes."

This divine panoply isn't metaphorical—it's spiritual technology of the highest order. The belt of truth holds our reality together when the enemy tries to unravel it with lies. The breastplate of righteousness shields our heart from the corruption that seeks to poison us from within. Our feet are shod with the gospel of peace, allowing us to stand firm when chaos threatens to sweep us away. The shield of faith doesn't just deflect the enemy's burning arrows—it extinguishes them completely. The helmet of salvation protects our minds from the psychological warfare of doubt and despair. And the sword of the Spirit—God's living Word—is the only offensive weapon we need, capable of cutting through every deception and darkness the Enemy can devise.

Each piece of this celestial armor resonates with divine purpose, forged in the fires of eternal truth. The Belt of Truth is more than just a declaration of truth; it represents our dynamic relationship

# THE BOY FROM BRAZIL

with Christ Himself, who declared, "I am the Truth." This belt holds our entire spiritual armor in place, just as our relationship with Jesus anchors every aspect of our faith journey. Without it, everything else falls away.

The breastplate of righteousness gleams not with our own goodness but with the radiant gift of Christ's perfection, bestowed upon us in that moment of surrender when we accepted Him as Lord. It covers our heart—our spiritual core—with His impenetrable righteousness, deflecting every accusation the Enemy hurls our way.

Our feet, shod with the readiness of the gospel, carry us sure-footed through the battlefield of this world. Like a warrior's sandals gripping treacherous terrain, this preparation keeps us steady as we share God's truth with others, turning each step of our journey into holy ground.

The Shield of Faith stands as our unwavering trust in God's character and promises, our undivided devotion raised high against the Enemy's fiery assaults. When doubt pours down like fiery arrows, this shield not only blocks but also extinguishes every flame of uncertainty with the soothing waters of divine faithfulness.

The Helmet of Salvation guards our minds against the Enemy's most insidious attacks, while the Sword of the Spirit—God's living Word—becomes a lightning bolt of truth in our hands, capable of piercing the darkest deceptions. Together, they form not just a defensive barrier but a complete arsenal for spiritual victory, transforming us from victims into warriors in this cosmic battle for souls.

## Points for Reflection

1. Do you believe there is any sin so great that God cannot forgive it? Reflect on what the Bible teaches about forgiveness and how this shapes your understanding of God's grace and mercy.

2. How can we live our lives as a response to God's grace and the gift of salvation? What actions, attitudes, or changes in behavior demonstrate gratitude for His forgiveness?

3. Think of a time in your life when you felt completely hopeless. What helped you find strength, and how was God present in your journey to overcome it?

# Chapter 6

---

# The Breakthrough

*"Behold, I stand at the door and knock. If anyone hears my voice and opens the door, I will come in and eat with him, and he with me."*

*Revelation 3:20*

### Prodigal's Journey

What echoes haunt the hollow man,
The child's voice that screams where wisdom ran?

Four decades adrift in somnambulant haze,
A puzzle piece lost in life's endless maze.
Untethered, unbound, too young to know
The cost of freedom's wild undertow.

Chasing mirages through gilded streets,

## THE BOY FROM BRAZIL                103

Scattering fortune like autumn leaves.
Each indulgence a compass pointing nowhere—
This wasteland was never his soul's prayer.

Though crowds pressed close, solitude grew,
Lost in wilderness, threading memories through
Labyrinths of smoke and shattered glass,
Where truth and illusion blindly pass.

When dreams lay broken in dawn's pale light,
Who held him through the endless night?
What voice could reach the child within,
Buried beneath years of wandering sin?

Blind to the beauty of his creation,
Heart sealed like a tomb in isolation,
Until surrender broke the spell—
Divine love tolling like a bell.

In morning's grace, he rose anew,
Shattered idols wet with dew.
From battlefield's wreckage, he turned away,
No longer would the prodigal stray.

From swine-filled depths and heaven's grief,
Rose psalms of joy, divine relief.
Running home on grace-swept ground,
Where father's arms at last were found.

In halls where celebration bloomed,

Ancient wounds were finally pruned.
Yet jealous eyes in shadows danced,
Where envy's serpents coiled, entranced.

Through hollow smiles and masquerade,
Sharp whispers cut like razor blade.
But nothing touched the peace within
Where grace had washed away all sin.

Beyond their lines of scripted praise,
Beyond their judgment's tangled maze,
The child within found holy rest,
In arms of love, divinely blessed.

For in surrender, truth unfolds:
The Father's love breaks earthly molds,
Teaching dreamers how to see
The sacred in simplicity.

Through time's long vigil, Love kept watch,
Till prodigal feet found sacred ground at last.

## A Jornada do Pródigo

Que ecos assombram o homem vazio,
A voz da criança que grita onde a sabedoria partiu?

Quatro décadas à deriva em névoa sonâmbula,

## THE BOY FROM BRAZIL

Uma peça perdida no labirinto infinito da vida.
Sem amarras, sem limites, jovem demais para saber
O preço da liberdade selvagem a se perder.

Perseguindo miragens por ruas douradas,
Desperdiçando fortuna como folhas outonadas.
Cada indulgência uma bússola sem direção—
Este deserto jamais foi o anseio do coração.

Embora multidões se aproximassem, a solidão crescia,
Perdido na vastidão, tecendo memórias que havia
Em labirintos de fumaça e vidros quebrados,
Onde verdade e ilusão passam vendados.

Quando sonhos se quebraram na luz da aurora,
Quem o segurou durante a noite afora?
Que voz poderia alcançar a criança interior,
Enterrada sob anos de pecado e dor?

Cego à beleza de sua criação,
Coração selado em isolamento e aflição,
Até que a rendição quebrou o feitiço—
Amor divino soando como um aviso.

Na graça da manhã,
ele renasceu,Ídolos quebrados molhados de orvalho ao céu.
Do campo de batalha em ruínas se afastou,
Não mais o filho pródigo vagou.

Das profundezas suínas e do luto celestial,

Ergueram-se salmos de alegria, alívio divinal.
Correndo para casa em solo de graça ungido,
Onde os braços do pai foram enfim encontrados.

Nos salões onde a celebração florescia,
Antigas feridas finalmente se guareciam.
Mas olhos invejosos nas sombras dançavam,
Onde serpentes da inveja se enrolavam.

Por sorrisos ocos e mascarada,
Sussurros cortantes como lâmina afiada.
Mas nada tocava a paz interior
Onde a graça lavou todo o torpor.

Além de seus louvores ensaiados,
Além de seus julgamentos emaranhados,
A criança interior encontrou santo descanso,
Nos braços do amor, divinamente manso.

Pois na rendição, a verdade se revela:
O amor do Pai quebra moldes terrenos com cautela,
Ensinando sonhadores como ver
O sagrado na simplicidade do ser.

Através da longa vigília, o Amor velou,
Até que os pés pródigos em solo sagrado encontrou.

In the hollow quiet of December 26th, in those liminal hours between Christmas joy and ordinary time, I awakened to darkness so profound it seemed alive. The familiar shadows of my bedroom

# THE BOY FROM BRAZIL

had transformed into something else entirely—a vast, velvet emptiness that pulsed with unseen presence. The darkness wasn't just an absence of light; it was a canvas waiting to be filled. In that moment, suspended between sleep and waking, between the old life and what was to come, I felt it: a divine stirring in the void, like the first tremors before an earthquake that would shake my world to its foundations.

Through that sacred darkness came not a voice, not a vision, but a touch—the unmistakable hand of God reaching across the infinite to rest upon my heart. Like lightning striking water, His presence rippled through every fiber of my being. The message He brought transcended language, bypassing my mind to speak directly to my soul. It was knowledge beyond knowing, certainty beyond proof. Just as a monarch butterfly navigates thousands of miles to a mountain it has never seen, guided by an invisible force woven into its very being, I knew with unshakeable clarity that God had found me and had chosen this ordinary night to write His extraordinary truth upon my heart.

Though physically alone in that midnight sanctuary of my bedroom, I was enveloped in a presence more real than any earthly companion. As the magnitude of this divine visitation crashed over me like waves breaking against ancient shores, something deep within me fractured and then reformed. For two hours, I wept with an intensity that shook my entire being—not tears of sorrow, but of transformation. They fell like holy rain, each drop carrying away fragments of my old self, washing clean years of accumulated darkness. These weren't just my tears; they were God's healing waters flowing through me. I was drowning and being saved all at once, caught in a spiritual undertow that pulled me toward a shore I couldn't yet see. In that moment of exquisite vulnerability, I was being remade, though I had yet to understand the profound metamorphosis taking place within my soul.

What divine alchemy was this? My mind grasped for understanding like a drowning man reaches for air, but explanations dissolved like mist in morning light. Though I stood in the eye of this spiritual storm, witnessing my own transformation, words failed to capture its essence. The experience defied the boundaries of human language—it was as impossible to describe as explaining color to the blind or music to the deaf. All I knew with certainty was that His touch had ignited something eternal within me, setting in motion a chain of events that would reshape the very foundation of my existence

## So Many Questions

Questions arose within me like incense smoke in a sacred temple—twisting, spiraling, impossible to grasp. Each answer I reached for dispersed into a thousand new mysteries. My thoughts turned to the faithful few—those friends and family who had lifted my name in prayer, their whispered supplications rising like invisible threads weaving a net of grace around me. Had their persistent prayers finally pierced the veil between heaven and earth? The notion offered a comforting logic, yet even as I considered it, I sensed that divine intervention defied such simple causation. How could human reasoning encompass this holy disruption of ordinary reality?

*"2. This man came to Jesus by night and said to him, 'Rabbi, we know that you are a teacher come from God, for no one can do these signs that you do unless God is with him.' 3. Jesus answered him, 'Truly, truly, I say to you, unless one is born again, he cannot see the kingdom of God.' 4. Nicodemus said to him, 'How can a man be born when he is old? Can he enter a second time into his mother's womb and be born?' 5. Jesus answered, 'Truly, truly, I say to you, unless one is born of water and the Spirit, he cannot enter the kingdom of God. 6. That which is*

*born of the flesh is flesh, and that which is born of the Spirit is spirit. 7. Do not marvel that I said to you, 'You must be born again.' 8. The wind blows where it wishes, and you hear its sound, but you do not know where it comes from or where it goes. So it is with everyone who is born of the Spirit.'"*

Here in this ancient exchange lay the key to my own midnight revelation. Like wind sweeping across desert sands, reshaping the landscape in its passing, the Spirit of God had moved through my room with sovereign freedom, answering prayers I hadn't even known were being prayed. In that sacred darkness, I was being unmade and remade—death and rebirth happening in the same eternal moment. The Kingdom of God wasn't just a distant promise or theological concept; it was breaking into my reality like dawn cracking open the night sky, its light spilling through every fissure in my carefully constructed world.

Like a pilgrim treading an ancient prayer labyrinth, I paced the confines of my home—kitchen to door, door to kitchen—my feet marking out a rhythm of reverence. From my lips spilled the only prayer my overwhelmed heart could form: "God is great." These words, simple yet profound, became my mantra, my anchor, my north star in this storm of divine revelation. With each repetition, the truth of those words crystallized more clearly, cutting through years of doubt like sunlight through fog. The phrase wasn't just a statement anymore—it was testimony, confession, and praise all at once. Every utterance felt like both an offering and an acknowledgment of my own smallness before His immensity

In that moment, Augustine's ancient words from his Confessions resonated through time to touch my soul: "Thou hast made us for thyself, O Lord, and our heart is restless until it finds its rest in thee." Suddenly, I understood this truth not just with my mind but with every fiber of my being. We were fashioned for this very purpose—to be vessels of worship, prisms through which His glory might shine. Though confusion still clouded much of my understanding, this one truth blazed like a beacon: God's greatness demanded response, and my soul had finally awakened to its primary purpose—worship. In my kitchen-turned-sanctuary, I was discovering what my heart had always known but my mind had long denied: that we are most fully alive when we are lost in wonder before His majesty.

## The Only Way Is Up: From Depths to Deliverance

The descent into darkness had been a slow erosion of hope, like water wearing away stone. Each day had carved new hollows of despair in my spirit, until I became a vessel filled only with doubt's bitter wine. In the depths of that darkness, even the concept of healing seemed like a cruel mirage—a shimmer of water in an endless desert. My story, I would come to understand, mirrored that of another seeker whose tale has echoed through millennia: the woman with the issue of blood, whose chronicle of suffering and eventual salvation in Luke 8:43-48 would become my own roadmap to redemption.

*"43. And there was a woman who had had a discharge of blood for twelve years, and though she had spent all her living on physicians, she could not be healed by anyone. 44. She came up behind him and touched the fringe of his garment, and immediately her discharge of blood ceased. 45. And Jesus said, 'Who was it that touched me?' When all denied it, Peter said, 'Master, the crowds surround you and are pressing in on you.' 46. But Jesus said, 'Someone touched me, for I perceive that power has gone out from me.' 47. And when the woman saw that she was not hidden, she came trembling, and falling down before him, declared in the presence of all the people why she had touched him and how she*

## THE BOY FROM BRAZIL

*had been immediately healed. 48. And he said to her, 'Daughter, your faith has made you well; go in peace.'"*

Consider the depths of her desperation—twelve years marked not by calendar pages but by endless attempts at healing, each failure cutting deeper than the last. Her wealth bled away like her life force, every failed remedy a new wound to her hope. Beyond the physical torment lay a deeper agony: her condition rendered her perpetually unclean under Levitical law, forcing her to wear her shame like a visible shroud. Each day brought fresh rejection, and each night new depths of isolation. Her existence had become a prison of impurity, her identity reduced to a walking embodiment of uncleanliness. Hope, that most resilient of human qualities, had nearly withered within her—until the day divine love took human form and walked her streets. In Jesus, she glimpsed what I too would discover: that rock bottom is not a place of ending but the foundation upon which God builds His most magnificent transformations.

Yet here lies the most exquisite truth about our Creator: He has woven into our very beings an eternal homing beacon, a divine GPS that pulses stronger the further we stray. Even in our darkest valleys, when we've wandered so far that hope seems a distant memory, this sacred signal continues its steady broadcast. It's as if God has placed within each human heart a spiritual compass whose needle, however violently shaken, always returns to point toward Him—our true magnetic north.

This divine positioning system operates outside time's constraints, for in our hearts, as in God's economy, all moments exist simultaneously: our past wanderings, our present struggles, and our future reconciliation are all known to Him. When we stray—and we all do—He doesn't abandon us to our wayward paths. Instead, like the most patient of navigators, He continuously recalculates our route home, sending gentle promptings through the static of our lives: a remembered scripture, a timely word from a friend, a moment of unexpected grace.

The story of Jonah stands as a testament to this relentless divine pursuit. Picture him, the reluctant prophet, charting a course directly opposite to God's calling, believing the vastness of the Mediterranean could hide him from his Creator's gaze. Yet even in the belly of the great fish—that living submarine of divine intervention—God's GPS never lost signal. Through storm and sea, through darkness and depth, the Almighty's purpose prevailed. The fish's belly became both Jonah's prison and his prayer room, his place of rebellion and his point of return. When finally deposited on that predestined shore, Jonah discovered what every wanderer eventually learns: that running from God only leads us, by circuitous routes, back to the path He originally marked out for us.

The pivot point between my old life and new came down to a single moment of surrender—as profound as it was simple. Like a drowning man finally ceasing his desperate thrashing to accept the lifeline extended from above, I made the decision to stop fighting against grace. The "fast life" I had been pursuing now revealed itself as an exhausting chase after shadows, while real substance—true life—had been waiting patiently for my return. Whether this transformation was catalyzed by others' prayers or my own desperate reaching toward heaven hardly mattered now. What mattered was the undeniable reality that everything—everything—was about to change.

Standing there in my home-turned-cathedral, still murmuring those words of praise, I felt time collapse in on itself. Past and present merged as memories surfaced with startling clarity, as if God himself were turning pages in the album of my life. The most vivid of these remembrances transported me back to childhood, to those Brazilian churches I had dismissed so casually. Back then, faith had seemed like an empty ritual, as meaningless as the dust motes dancing in the sunbeams that streamed through stained glass windows. But now, through the lens of this divine visitation, those memories took on new depth and significance.

These weren't mere recollections—they were visions, supernatural in their clarity and power. I could smell the musty sweetness of well-worn pew cushions, feel the smooth leather of that first Bible beneath my fingertips, and hear the distant echoes of Portuguese hymns floating through time. Every detail was crystalline, more vivid than any dream, as if God were showing me that He had been present even then, planting seeds that would lie dormant until this very moment of awakening. In His divine economy, nothing had been wasted—not even those years of apparent indifference.

The memories continued to unfold, carrying me back to that pivotal seventh year of life when I first grappled with questions of identity and purpose. I realized now that I had experienced a similar divine encounter then—a holy moment I had buried beneath years of worldly pursuit. But here in this sacred present, wrapped in God's presence like a warm cloak, time became fluid. His spirit acted as a divine archivist, allowing me to access not just memories but moments of alternate possibility—glimpses of the life I might have lived had I remained faithful to that first calling.

Then came the most extraordinary vision of all: I found myself ascending, weightless as morning mist, into the very courts of Heaven. The beloved hymn "I Surrender All" seemed to emanate not from any earthly source but from the very fabric of eternity itself, its familiar melody transformed into something ineffably sublime. Each note became a golden thread drawing me upward, each word a step on a stairway of light. This wasn't just imagination or religious reverie—it was a foretaste of glory divine, a glimpse behind the veil that separates temporal from eternal.

In that transcendent moment, I understood with stunning clarity that eternal life wasn't some distant reward to be claimed after death—it was a present reality breaking into my existence right now, transforming every molecule of my being. All earthly pleasures I had ever known—every triumph, every sensation, every moment of fleeting happiness—paled like stars at sunrise compared to this overwhelming peace. As Romans 5:8 declares, "Therefore, since we have been justified by faith, we have peace with God through our Lord Jesus Christ." This was that peace—not the world's temporary cease-fire between conflicts, but God's shalom, His supernatural completeness flooding every empty space in my soul.

## A Broken Compass: Navigation Without True North

In the years before this divine intervention, I had fashioned myself into a moral navigator, attempting to chart my own course through the treacherous waters of right and wrong. Like a sailor who decides to ignore the stars and rely solely on his own sense of direction, I had attempted to usurp God's role as the ultimate moral authority. This cosmic act of mutiny—trying to captain my own soul—was doomed from the start, as evidenced by the shipwrecks of poor choices littering my wake.

Now I understood with piercing clarity why the first prohibition in Eden centered on the Tree of the Knowledge of Good and Evil. This wasn't merely an arbitrary test of obedience; it was a fundamental truth about the nature of morality itself. Just as a compass needle can only function properly when aligned with the Earth's magnetic field, the human conscience can only navigate accurately when calibrated to its divine Creator. By attempting to determine good and evil for myself, I had been trying to generate my own magnetic field—an exercise in spiritual futility that left me spinning in endless circles of confusion.

The mystery of that ancient garden suddenly crystallized: God wasn't withholding knowledge out of jealousy or control, but out of love. He alone could be the fixed point by which all moral coordinates are measured. Evil, I now saw, wasn't merely the breaking of rules—it was the fundamental misalignment of the human heart from its true magnetic north. It was the futile attempt to navigate by our own light rather than by His stars.

In this misguided navigation, I had erected false lighthouses along treacherous shores. Chief among these deceptive beacons was my sexuality—an idol I had crafted from desire and desperate need for validation. Like ancient sailors lured onto rocks by siren songs, I had followed the seductive call of momentary pleasure, mistaking the intensity of passion for the depth of true fulfillment. Each fleeting encounter became another false harbor where I sought shelter from the storm of my own emptiness.

Paul's warning to the Philippian church now struck me with the force of prophecy fulfilled:

*"18. For many, of whom I have often told you and now tell you even with tears, walk as enemies of the cross of Christ. 19. Their end is destruction, their god is their belly, and they glory in their shame, with minds set on earthly things."*

In the harsh light of divine truth, I saw myself in Paul's tears. My god had been the insatiable appetite of desire, my glory found in things that should have brought shame. I had transformed the sacred gift of human sexuality into a golden calf, dancing around it in desperate worship while the true God waited patiently on His holy mountain.

The very capacity that should have pointed to His creative power—for we are made in His image, designed to reflect His nature—had become a distorting mirror, reflecting only my own brokenness. Like a compass needle magnetized to the wrong pole, I had consistently mistaken pleasure for goodness, desire for divine guidance.

Such self-determined morality was like trying to build a house on shifting sand—every foundation I laid crumbled beneath the weight of reality. The authority to define good and evil, to chart the course of human purpose, had never been mine to claim. These eternal truths were written in the very fabric of creation, authored by God himself. Only by surrendering my self-appointed role as architect of my own destiny and allowing the Master Builder to work could I begin to discover what love truly meant—not the counterfeit currency I had been trading in, but the pure gold of divine love.

The path ahead would demand more than mere course correction; it would require a complete reconstruction of my identity. Years of defining myself through the narrow lens of sexuality had left deep grooves in my psyche, like ancient ruts in a well-traveled road. My relationships had been transactions rather than connections, each party seeking to take rather than give, to fill their own emptiness with another's essence. Now I understood that genuine love—the kind that flows from Christ's heart—always seeks to pour itself out first, to give without calculating the return. Such love could only be found in those who had themselves been transformed by divine grace.

The suffering I had endured—though I had been too blind to recognize it as suffering—was like that of a man dying of thirst while swimming in salt water: surrounded by what seemed to be the answer, yet being destroyed by it. But that tear-soaked night of divine intervention had restored my spiritual vision, helping me see that God had never intended for me to thrash about in these bitter waters. Through

# THE BOY FROM BRAZIL                    117

His sacrificial love on Calvary, He had already provided the pure, living water I desperately needed. His cross stood as both lighthouse and lifeline, beckoning me from the darkness of self-determination into the radiant dawn of His purpose.

## Changing My Behavior: Digital Altars Torn Down

The dawn after my divine encounter brought with it the first test of my newfound clarity: my phone, that pocket-sized temple of modern idolatry, lay waiting. Each dating app icon glowed like an ember from my former life, promising connection but delivering only ash. With trembling fingers but a resolute heart, I began the digital demolition of my false altars. Each deletion felt like pulling down a stone from Babel's tower—my misguided attempt to reach heaven through human means crumbling one tap at a time.

The effect was immediate and profound. With each app that vanished from my screen, an invisible weight lifted from my spirit. These seemingly small actions carried the weight of ancient ritual—like Joshua removing the foreign gods from among the Israelites or Gideon destroying his father's altar to Baal. Though my fingers performed simple taps and swipes, in the spiritual realm, mountains were moving. Each deletion was both confession and proclamation: a renunciation of my digital idolatry and a declaration of trust in Christ's sufficiency.

For we are, I was learning, not merely shaped but sculpted by our choices. Each decision acts like a chisel stroke on the marble of our character, gradually revealing either the image of God or a grotesque counterfeit. Every previous choice to prioritize digital validation and instant gratification had carved me further from His likeness. But now, in this holy moment of digital purging, I was choosing a different kind of transformation. Each deleted app became a yes to Christ's invitation to "Come, follow me," each empty screen space a canvas for His restoring work.

In the wake of my spiritual rebirth came a journey that would test and affirm my transformation—a pilgrimage to Key West. This island, traditionally a symbol of hedonistic escape, had long been a beacon for those seeking to lose themselves in pleasure's numbing embrace. The very name conjured images of endless parties and spring break excess, a paradise of purposeful forgetting. But God, in His divine irony, chose this unlikely sanctuary for my first steps as a new creation.

The journey south felt like crossing a threshold between two worlds. With each mile marker counting down to zero, I was leaving behind not just geographical distance but spiritual territory as well. Where others came to Key West to escape reality, I had come to embrace a deeper truth. Where they sought to blur their vision with excess, I had come to see with newfound clarity.

What awaited me was nothing short of miraculous. Walking along shores that had witnessed countless stories of debauchery, I experienced a profound lightness of being. My feet seemed to barely disturb the sand, as if the very gravity of my old life had lost its hold. Like the butterfly emerging from its chrysalis—still damp-winged and trembling with new possibility—I found myself suspended between earth and heaven, held aloft by grace. God's presence, far from fading in this place of former temptation, grew more palpable with each step.

The ocean itself seemed transformed through the lens of my redemption. Those famous turquoise waters, which had once served as a backdrop for countless scenes of excess, now reflected divine artistry. Each wave appeared as polished crystal, not the sharp-edged kind that cuts and wounds, but smooth-worn pieces of heaven's own architecture. The rhythmic surf became a lullaby of grace, each breaker a testament to God's endless creativity and love. As 2 Corinthians 5:17

# THE BOY FROM BRAZIL

declares, "Therefore, if anyone is in Christ, he is a new creation. The old has passed away; behold, the new has come"—and here, in this transformed paradise, I felt the full weight of that promise in every salt-kissed breeze.

Standing there on Key West's shore, my mind drifted to that powerful final scene in "The Pursuit of Happyness"—Will Smith's character finally achieving his breakthrough after months of grinding poverty and desperation. Those tears he shed weren't just relief at finding success; they were the holy water of redemption, washing away months of struggle and fear. In that moment, I understood his emotion at a soul-deep level. My own pursuit of happiness had been a longer odyssey—years spent chasing fulfillment down all the wrong paths, searching for love in empty encounters, seeking validation in hollow victories.

But now, bathed in the golden light of God's grace on this transformed shoreline, I felt what Christopher Gardner must have felt in that moment of triumph: the exquisite recognition that all the pain had served a purpose, that every dark night had been leading to this dawn. The tears that slipped down my cheeks tasted of both salt and sweetness—the bitter waters of my past transformed into the wine of new life.

Standing at this spiritual milestone, I knew with bone-deep certainty that there could be no return to my former life. Just as a butterfly cannot crawl back into its chrysalis once its wings have unfurled, I could never again squeeze my transformed soul into the confines of my old existence. The door to that life hadn't just closed; it had vanished, replaced by an open gateway to unimagined possibilities in Christ.

The second journey proved to be an even more profound test of my transformation. Miami beckoned—not the sun-drenched city of postcards, but the neon-lit realm of endless nightlife where I'd once sought hollow communion. My friends, still devoted disciples of the night, saw the city as their pleasure dome, a temple of perpetual celebration. But I was no longer a congregant of that faith. While agreeing to accompany them, I drew a clear line in the sand: I would be present but not participate in the old rituals of pursuit and conquest.

Stepping into the club felt like entering a spiritual war zone. Strobing lights pierced the artificial fog like arrows, while the bass thundered like distant artillery. This was the antithesis of the divine peace I'd found in Key West—a cacophonous assault on the senses that seemed designed to drown out the still, small voice I'd learned to cherish. The atmosphere was thick with more than just smoke; it was heavy with desperate desires and unfulfilled longings, a tangible darkness that pressed against my newly awakened spirit.

Seeking refuge, I ascended a flight of stairs to a crowded balcony. What happened next could only be described as supernatural: as I approached, the crowd parted like the Red Sea before Moses, creating a path to the railing. It wasn't mere coincidence or polite deference—there was a palpable force at work, as if invisible hands were clearing sacred space in this profane temple. Standing at that elevated vantage point, looking down at the swirling mass of humanity below, I felt like Elijah on Mount Carmel, surrounded by worshippers of a different god.

In that moment, I lifted up a silent prayer, letting it rise above the thundering music like incense. The same smoke that had once obscured my vision now seemed to form a protective curtain around me. Drawing upon words that had become my anchor, I claimed the promise of Psalm 28:7: "The Lord is my strength and my shield; in him my heart trusts, and I am helped; my heart exults, and with my song I give thanks to him." In this modern Babylon, God himself had

# THE BOY FROM BRAZIL

become my fortress, my shield against the siren songs that had once held me captive.

As my prayer ascended through the haze, something extraordinary began to happen. A divine current seemed to flow through my body, from crown to sole, like electricity seeking ground. My physical form became a vessel for something far greater than myself—a sacred conduit for divine presence. My tongue, no longer under my own governance, began forming words I had never learned yet somehow knew in the deepest part of my being. The ancient promise of Isaiah 50:4 was being fulfilled in real time: "The Lord GOD has given me the tongue of those who are taught, that I may know how to sustain with a word him who is weary."

Through my lips came words of startling clarity and power: "Look at my people," His voice spoke through me, "Look at how everybody missed the whole meaning of life and identity." From my elevated perspective, the scene below took on prophetic significance. The writhing crowd, the desperate pursuit of connection through chemistry and rhythm, the hollow echoes of laughter—all of it suddenly appeared in sharp spiritual focus, like scales falling from my eyes. I saw what I had been before: another blind soul stumbling through the dark, mistaking shadows for substance.

The words of 2 Corinthians 4:4 illuminated the scene with terrible clarity: "In their case the god of this world has blinded the minds of the unbelievers, to keep them from seeing the light of the gospel of the glory of Christ, who is the image of God." Looking down from that balcony-turned-prophet's-perch, I witnessed the truth of this scripture played out in living tableau. Each person below was like I had been—eyes darkened to divine reality, seeking life in places of death, trying to fill God-shaped voids with human-shaped solutions. The tragedy and beauty of it broke my heart: tragedy for their current blindness, beauty in knowing that the same light that had pierced my darkness could illuminate theirs.

As divine presence receded like an ebbing tide, those prophetic words continued to reverberate through my being: "Look how everybody missed the whole meaning of life and identity." They echoed not just in my ears but in the marrow of my bones, each repetition carving deeper channels of truth in my consciousness. There, amid the pulsing rhythms of Miami nightlife, I made a covenant with God as binding as any ancient sacrifice. This was my personal altar-building moment, my burning-bush encounter, my Jacob-at-Bethel commitment.

The words formed in my heart with crystal clarity: Wherever You lead, I will follow. Whatever You command, I will obey. My life would still be my own—God doesn't create puppets—but it would be lived in harmony with His divine orchestration rather than the discordant rhythms of flesh. The chains of lust that had once bound me now lay broken at my feet, shattered by a power greater than my own desires.

In that electric moment of surrender, it was as if I gained access to a higher dimension of self-awareness. I saw myself with unprecedented clarity—not just the external facade I presented to the world, but the inner landscape of my soul being transformed by divine grace. Like a masterpiece being restored to its original brilliance, layers of accumulated grime were being stripped away to reveal God's true design underneath. As I prepared to leave Miami, not a shadow of doubt darkened my spirit. The God who had orchestrated this transformation would remain my constant companion, my divine GPS, my ever-present help in continuing this journey of redemption.

Yet divine transformation, I would soon learn, is not a passive metamorphosis. The butterfly may emerge from its chrysalis by God's design, but it must still struggle against that shell to strengthen its wings

THE BOY FROM BRAZIL                                          123

for flight. The question arose in my spirit with sobering clarity: Would this profound encounter automatically reshape my entire existence?

The answer thundered back with the force of conviction: Absolutely not! This divine intervention was not a magical spell that would automatically reorder my life, but rather a call to holy participation in my own redemption. Like the Israelites who had to physically walk out of Egypt even after God had spiritually freed them, I now faced the demanding journey of practical obedience. The theoretical beauty of transformation had to be worked out in the crucible of daily choices.

First among these choices was the painful but necessary pruning of relationships. Like a garden overtaken by invasive vines, my life had become entangled with connections that would strangle any new growth toward heaven. Each friendship rooted in the soil of my former life would need to be carefully evaluated and, in many cases, lovingly but firmly severed. The words of 1 Peter 4:4 rang with prophetic resonance: "With respect to this they are surprised when you do not join them in the same flood of debauchery, and they malign you." I could already anticipate the bewildered looks, the hurt accusations, and the subtle and not-so-subtle attempts to pull me back into familiar patterns of sin. But like a recovering addict who must avoid old haunts and habits, I knew that true freedom would require radical amputation of anything that might drag me back into the prison of lust.

## Change Isn't Easy: The Price of Transformation

The path of transformation, I soon discovered, was paved with both triumph and tears. Each step forward brought its own peculiar kind of ache—a holy pain that felt both destructive and creative, like a sculptor's chisel reshaping stone. When the time came to have those difficult conversations with friends who had been part of my former life, every shared laugh we'd ever had seemed to echo accusingly in my memory. Each smile we'd exchanged became a weight on my heart. These weren't just casual acquaintances I was leaving behind; they were fellow travelers on my journey thus far, human beings created in God's image, even if their paths could no longer parallel mine.

Perhaps even more challenging than severing these external connections was confronting the internal damage I had inflicted upon myself. Like an archaeologist excavating ruins, I had to carefully unearth years of emotional debris, examining each painful artifact of my past choices. Every casual encounter that had chipped away at my soul's capacity for genuine intimacy, every relationship that had left scar tissue where healthy attachment should have grown—all of it demanded acknowledgment and grieving.

This process unveiled another profound spiritual paradox: I had to make peace with a past I could no longer embrace. The years spent wandering in my personal wilderness, far from God's love and light, couldn't simply be erased or ignored. They were part of my story, threads in the tapestry of my testimony. Yet while acknowledging these chapters of my life, I couldn't allow myself to become like Lot's wife, turned to a pillar of salt by looking back at what I was leaving behind. The delicate balance between healthy reflection and paralyzing regret became my daily meditation.

The weight of my past demanded a double portion of forgiveness—from God and from myself. Like two keys needed to unlock a sacred vault, both were essential for my liberation. God's forgiveness had been freely given at Calvary, but accepting it, truly believing in its completeness, required a daily renewal of faith. Self-forgiveness proved the more elusive key, requiring me to view my past through the lens of divine grace rather than human shame.

## THE BOY FROM BRAZIL

Paul's words to the Philippians became my spiritual north star in this journey:

*"13. Brothers, I do not consider that I have made it my own. But one thing I do: forgetting what lies behind and straining forward to what lies ahead, 14. I press on toward the goal for the prize of the upward call of God in Christ Jesus."*

Yet before I could fully embrace this forward momentum, I had to confront the fundamental misunderstandings that had shaped my former life. Chief among these was my distorted view of beauty and worth. I had been like a man standing in an art gallery, fixated on my reflection in the protective glass rather than the masterpieces behind it. My obsession with physical appearance—forever seeking validation in mirrors and polished surfaces—now seemed like a tragic comedy of errors. While the human body is indeed a marvel of divine engineering, a testament to God's creative genius, I had mistaken the frame for the painting, the vessel for its contents.

The irony was crushing: in my pursuit of physical beauty and sexual conquest, I had become spiritually blind to life's true splendor. Like a man dying of thirst while floating on an ocean, my lust had rendered me unable to perceive the vast ocean of divine love surrounding me. This blindness hadn't just robbed me of earthly joy—it had obscured my view of eternity itself, that grand canvas upon which God paints with the colors of forever.

At the heart of my transformation lay a profound revelation: my journey into darkness had begun not with rebellion, but with ignorance. Like a butterfly unaware of its own magnificent design, I had been blind to both my divine worth and my destructive choices. This spiritual blindness had led me step by step into idolatry, much as a person walking in darkness might unknowingly wander from a safe path into treacherous terrain. I had been given the gift of freedom but, like a child with a powerful tool, had wielded it without wisdom or understanding. The words of Galatians 5:13 now illuminated this truth with piercing clarity: "For you were called to freedom, brothers. Only do not use your freedom as an opportunity for the flesh, but through love serve one another."

This understanding brought with it a second, equally crucial revelation: the necessity of extending grace to my former self. The path to genuine transformation required me to lay down not just my sins, but also the whip of self-condemnation with which I had been flagellating myself. True repentance, I was learning, meant accepting full responsibility for my choices while simultaneously accepting God's full forgiveness for them. It meant standing in the light of truth without allowing that light to burn me with shame.

The final frontier of change proved to be the most nuanced: I had to evolve into someone who could look back at my former self not with disgust or dismissal, but with the same compassionate understanding that Christ had shown to tax collectors and sinners. This meant developing the spiritual maturity to hate the sin while truly loving the sinner—even when that sinner was my past self. Like a parent looking at childhood photos of their now-grown child, I needed to view my former self with a mixture of honest acknowledgment and gentle understanding, recognizing both the brokenness and the beloved child of God in that previous version of me.

In this season of transformation, the Parable of the Prodigal Son (Luke 15:11-32) became more than just a familiar story—it became a mirror reflecting my own journey home. Like that wayward son, I had come to recognize not just the external consequences of my choices but their deeper spiritual implications. Yet the parable held a subtle truth I had never before noticed: the son's return required not only physical movement toward home but also a profound shift in

# THE BOY FROM BRAZIL

self-perception. Had he remained trapped in self-loathing, he might never have found the courage to face his father.

My Miami experience had brought me to a similar crossroads. The initial recognition of my spiritual poverty, while crucial, was only the beginning. I had to learn a new way of speaking to myself—not the harsh condemnation that could drive me back to the pig pen of my former life, nor the casual dismissal of sin's severity, but rather the balanced truth-telling of grace. The common phrase "love the sinner but hate the sin" took on deeply personal meaning when I became both the one loving and the one being loved.

This delicate balance of honest acknowledgment and gracious acceptance became my daily practice. Like a tightrope walker holding the pole of truth in one hand and grace in the other, I learned to navigate the narrow path between minimizing my past sins and being defined by them. Each step forward required both unflinching honesty about where I had been and unshakeable faith in where God was leading me. This holy tension—this divine paradox of being both fully known and fully loved—finally allowed me to integrate my past into the larger narrative God was writing with my life.

## Forgiveness and the Church: Finding Sacred Community

The river of forgiveness that had begun to flow through my life soon led to an unexpected tributary: a renewed understanding of church. Like many spiritual wanderers, I had long dismissed the institution of church as an unnecessary middleman in my relationship with God. In my childhood, the very concept had seemed like an antiquated ritual, a relic of less enlightened times. "Why do I need a building to talk to God?" my younger self had demanded. "What's wrong with praying in my bedroom?" These questions, once posed with adolescent defiance, now revealed themselves as evidence of my spiritual immaturity.

The transformation of my understanding was as dramatic as my personal conversion. Church, I began to realize, was never meant to be merely a physical location for worship, any more than a home is merely a shelter from the elements. Just as a house becomes a home through the relationships it nurtures, a church building becomes the Church through the sacred community it hosts. This was the profound truth I had missed in my years of spiritual isolation: while God can indeed be worshipped anywhere, there is something uniquely powerful about joining your voice with others who have also been touched by grace.

My previous objections now seemed like someone refusing to attend family dinners because they could eat alone in their room. Yes, the basic function of nourishment could be accomplished in solitude, but such isolation missed the deeper purpose of communion—both with God and with fellow believers. The Church, I was discovering, was not a building but a body, not an institution but an organism, alive with the breath of the Spirit and pulsing with the shared heartbeat of redeemed sinners.

Though my own Damascus Road experience had occurred in the solitude of my bedroom rather than within sacred walls, I soon discovered that the church offered something essential to my spiritual growth. It became a weekly wellspring of renewal, a sacred space where the initial flame of my conversion could be steadily fanned into a sustainable fire. Like a garden carefully tended, my relationship with God found rich soil and regular nourishment within the community of believers. The same God who had reached down to me in my darkness now reached out through the hands and hearts of fellow pilgrims on the journey.

## THE BOY FROM BRAZIL

The church became my spiritual gymnasium, where the muscles of faith could be strengthened through regular exercise of worship, prayer, and fellowship. Here, the love that God had so freely poured into my life could be practiced and multiplied in community. What I had once dismissed as an unnecessary institution revealed itself as a divine incubator for spiritual growth, a greenhouse where tender shoots of new faith could be protected and nurtured into sturdy plants.

After four decades of wandering in the wilderness of self-reliance and false identity, this revelation felt like stepping into a promised land of authentic community. The contrast was stark: where once I had exhausted myself trying to construct a facade of worthiness through physical appearance and sexual conquest, now I could simply be—fully known, fully accepted, fully loved. In this sacred space, holiness wasn't a burden to bear but a natural outgrowth of genuine relationship with God and His people. My church became not just a building I visited but a vital part of my identity, a community where I could finally live out the authentic self God had always intended me to be.

As my faith deepened, both within the sanctuary walls and beyond them, I discovered that my spiritual awakening had heightened all my senses. It was as if God had given me new eyes and ears—not just for Him, but for others as well. When people spoke, I found myself hearing beyond their words to the subtle harmonics of their hearts' unspoken longings. This new capacity for empathy and understanding felt like a divine gift, replacing my former self-absorbed fog with crystal clarity. Where anxiety and restless questioning had once created constant static in my mind, now peace flowed like a steady stream, washing away the debris of my former life of misplaced worship.

This growing spiritual awareness began to illuminate areas of my life that no longer aligned with my new identity in Christ. My workplace, in particular, stood out like a jarring discord in an otherwise harmonious symphony. The verbal abuse and toxic atmosphere I had long endured now revealed themselves as not just personally harmful, but spiritually incongruent. With startling clarity, I realized that accepting such treatment wasn't just about me anymore—it was about dishonoring the God whose image I bore.

The revelation struck me with the force of divine logic: if God Himself had deemed me worthy of Christ's sacrifice, who was I to accept treatment that contradicted that worth? Every instance of allowing myself to be diminished or abused wasn't just personal passivity—it was a tacit denial of my status as God's beloved child. The same divine love that compelled me to treat others with respect demanded that I extend that same respect to myself. After all, I too was fearfully and wonderfully made, crafted in the image of the Creator with an inherent dignity that no human had the right to trample.

This wasn't pride or self-importance; it was simply good stewardship of the vessel God had entrusted to my care. Just as a masterful painting deserves proper protection and display, my life—now recognized as a canvas for God's ongoing work—required an environment worthy of its divine purpose.

In this new season of spiritual clarity, I brought my workplace struggles before God's throne, simply asking for His direction. His response was swift and decisive—doors began opening almost immediately, job offers appearing like spring flowers after rain. As I stepped into new professional territory, I felt like Moses viewing the promised land from Mount Nebo, seeing the contours of a better future spread out before me. But this career change was merely the first domino in a cascade of transformation that would reshape every aspect of my existence.

# THE BOY FROM BRAZIL

The renovation of my life was total and uncompromising. Like a house being gutted for complete restoration, nearly everything familiar was stripped away. My social circle contracted dramatically as former friendships, built on shared pursuits of pleasure rather than purpose, naturally fell away. My daily routines, once centered around self-gratification, were demolished and rebuilt around spiritual disciplines and authentic connections. If someone had described this life to my younger self—a life marked by simplicity, spiritual focus, and genuine peace—I would have dismissed it as boring at best, impossible at worst. The me of my twenties and thirties, still chasing the neon lights of temporal pleasure, couldn't have comprehended the profound satisfaction found in spiritual authenticity.

Most significantly, my approach to relationships underwent a complete paradigm shift. Instead of evaluating connections through the lens of personal gratification—what can this person do for me?—I began applying a higher standard: how does this relationship affect my walk with God? Like a skilled gardener carefully selecting which plants to cultivate in limited soil, I became intentional about nurturing only those relationships that would bear spiritual fruit. This wasn't cold calculation, but rather wise stewardship of emotional and spiritual resources. As Jesus taught us to seek first the kingdom of God, I learned to prioritize my relationship with Him above all else. Like a butterfly instinctively drawn to the most nourishing nectar, my heart had finally found its true sustenance in communion with the Divine.

## Different Strokes for Different Folks: Walking the Narrow Path

One of the most sobering revelations of my spiritual journey emerged gradually: the path I now walked would often be a solitary one. Like Noah building an ark under clear skies, my new life choices and perspectives frequently met with bewildered stares and subtle mockery. Even the most casual mention of faith could transform ordinary conversations into awkward silences, while deeper sharing about my relationship with God often elicited reactions ranging from polite dismissal to outright skepticism.

This social disconnect wasn't just about religious differences—it reflected a fundamental shift in worldview that created an invisible but palpable barrier between my new life and the old world I had left behind. It was as if I now spoke a language that many of my former associates couldn't comprehend, seeing colors they couldn't perceive. Their inability to understand wasn't necessarily hostility; it was more like trying to describe sunrise to someone who had lived their entire life underground.

The temptation to water down my testimony or keep my transformation private was real and persistent. Yet I remembered how Jesus himself faced incomprehension and rejection, even from his own hometown. The same Savior who warned that the path to life was narrow and few would find it had also experienced the loneliness of being misunderstood. While my heart yearned for everyone to experience the profound peace and purpose I had found in Christ, I had to accept that spiritual awakening was a deeply personal journey that each soul must undertake in its own time, if at all.

Yet the magnificent truth that sustains me is this: God towers infinitely above human skepticism and doubt. His divine timeline operates independently of human understanding or approval. When He determines the moment is right for transformation in a life, that sovereign decision supersedes all earthly opposition. Like a master sculptor, He uses every trial and tribulation as a chisel, every challenge as sandpaper, carefully crafting us into vessels worthy of His purpose. The process of removing damaging influences from our lives may feel like spiritual surgery without anesthesia—painful but necessary for healing.

Through each phase of this divine reconstruction, He maintains intimate communication with His beloved. Sometimes through scripture, sometimes through circumstances, sometimes through that still, small voice that speaks directly to the heart—He consistently reassures us of His presence. The ancient promise of Isaiah 41:10 reverberates through time to comfort every seeking soul: "Fear not, for I am with you; be not dismayed, for I am your God; I will strengthen you, I will help you, I will uphold you with my righteous right hand."

Like a butterfly that seems fragile yet can navigate thousand-mile migrations by drawing strength from flower to flower, I have learned to derive my sustenance from daily communion with God. Each morning's devotion, each moment of prayer, and each act of worship become nectar for the soul, fueling this extraordinary journey of faith. Though it took four decades of wandering to reach this understanding, my heart overflows with gratitude for the persistence of a God who never stopped pursuing me, never stopped believing in the person I could become in Him. The length of the journey only serves to sweeten its completion, making every step—even the painful ones—worth the wait.

## Reflecting on Breakthrough Moments

Take a moment to contemplate your own spiritual journey. What divine breakthrough stands as a watershed moment in your relationship with God? Consider not just the event itself, but its timing and context. Why do you think God chose that particular moment to intervene so powerfully? Remember that divine responses rarely follow our human timetables or logic.

Many believers fall into the trap of viewing prayer as a spiritual vending machine—insert the right combination of words and actions, receive the desired result. But God's wisdom far exceeds our limited understanding of cause and effect. Sometimes His seeming silence speaks volumes, and His delays often serve as protection or preparation for something greater than we initially sought.

## Understanding True Prayer

While we often reduce prayer to a mere wish list presented to the Divine, its true essence runs far deeper. Yes, the dictionary defines prayer as "a solemn request for help or expression of thanks addressed to God," but this clinical description barely scratches the surface of what genuine communion with the Creator entails. Prayer is the heartbeat of our relationship with God—a dynamic, two-way connection that encompasses:

This is also the reason why we will not be disappointed if our prayers are not answered. Since we fully trust God, His plan for us is always way better. When we have a developing, growing, and healthy relationship with God, that is a true breakthrough.

## The Living Relationship

At its core, Christianity transcends the boundaries of mere religion—it is a vibrant, living relationship with the Creator of the universe. Like any meaningful relationship, it requires intentional nurturing through consistent, authentic communication. This divine dialogue operates on multiple frequencies: God speaks primarily through His written Word, the Bible, but also through circumstances, other believers, and the gentle whispers of His Spirit. We, in turn, communicate through prayer, worship, and obedient action.

## The Art of Divine Dialogue

The depth of our prayer life directly correlates with the intimacy of our relationship with God. As we grow in knowing Him, our prayers naturally evolve from timid requests to bold declarations of faith. Hebrews 4:16 captures this beautiful progression: "Let us then approach God's throne of grace with confidence, so that we may receive mercy and find grace to help us in our time of need." This confidence isn't presumption—it's the natural outcome of growing trust, like a child who approaches their father without hesitation, knowing they are deeply loved and understood.

## Aligning with Divine Will

The effectiveness of our prayers isn't measured by their eloquence but by their alignment with God's will. As 1 John 5:14-15 assures us: "This is the confidence we have in approaching God: that if we ask anything according to his will, he hears us. And if we know that he hears us—whatever we ask—we know that we have what we asked of him." This remarkable promise hinges on knowing God's character and desires so intimately that our requests naturally flow from His heart through ours. It's less about getting God to align with our will and more about discovering the joy of aligning ourselves with His perfect plans.

## Learning from the Master of Prayer

In Jesus Christ, we find the supreme model of prayer—not just in its practice, but in its priority. His example offers us a masterclass in divine communion, showing us that even the Son of God prioritized these sacred conversations with the Father. Mark 1:35 provides a glimpse into His prayer routine: "Very early in the morning, while it was still dark, Jesus got up, left the house, and went off to a solitary place, where he prayed."

This simple verse reveals several profound insights about effective prayer:

- **Intentional Timing**: Jesus chose the predawn hours, before the demands of ministry could crowd out His communion with the Father. In the quiet darkness, when the world still slept, He carved out sacred space for divine dialogue.

- **Physical Separation**: By leaving the house and finding a solitary place, Jesus demonstrated the importance of creating both physical and mental space for prayer. Sometimes, drawing closer to God requires stepping away from familiar surroundings.

- **Consistent Priority**: Despite knowing the crushing demands that each day would bring—teaching, healing, deal-

# THE BOY FROM BRAZIL

ing with crowds, training disciples—Jesus never allowed these important activities to supersede His most important relationship. Prayer wasn't something He squeezed into His schedule; it was the foundation upon which His schedule was built.

This pattern reveals a profound truth: if Jesus Himself, being fully divine, saw such vital importance in regular, intimate prayer with the Father, how much more crucial must it be for us, His followers, to cultivate similar habits of devotion?

## Points for Reflection

1. "Describe a time when God answered your prayers in an unexpected way. How did this experience transform your understanding of faith and divine timing?"

2. "What ongoing prayers or spiritual desires have you been bringing before God? How has the waiting period affected your relationship with Him and shaped your spiritual growth?"

3. "When facing what seems like divine silence or 'no' as an answer, how do you maintain your faith? What spiritual practices or biblical teachings help you trust God's wisdom in these moments?"

# Chapter 7

# Holy Identify

*"It is in the quiet crucible of your personal private sufferings that your noblest dreams are born and God's greatest gifts are given in compensation for what you have been through."*
*- Wintley Phipps*

*"At the intersection where your gifts, talents, and abilities meet a human need; therein you discover your purpose."*
*- Aristotle*

Like ships lost in a tempest, we often find ourselves swept away by the relentless waves of modern life until the shores of our true identity fade from view. The world's cacophony—its glittering distractions and siren songs—slowly erodes the bedrock of who we truly are. 2 Peter 1:9 says, "But whoever does not have these qualities is nearsighted and blind, forgetting that they have been cleansed from their past sins." This spiritual amnesia becomes a cruel cycle, each forgotten redemption leading us back into the same shadowed valleys we once escaped.

The world beckons with honey-sweet promises, tempting us to believe we can navigate its waters without our divine compass. Yet

# THE BOY FROM BRAZIL                    139

deep within, like a lodestone forever drawn north, our souls yearn for their Creator. No matter how far we drift into secular seas, that spiritual magnetism remains, pulling us toward home. No matter how we occupy ourselves with sin, we will always need to return to the root of our existence. Perhaps God, in His infinite wisdom, allows us to wander into these spiritual deserts so we might truly understand the oasis of His presence. He wants us to understand the falsity that living according to the desires of the world is better than living under Him. We are innately compelled, like salmon returning to their natal streams despite overwhelming challenges, to find our path back to God. It is an impulse that simply is part of our human nature. It is who we are and how He made us.

## Losing Identity to Desires and Awakening

The moment we sever our communion with God, our sense of self begins to unravel like a tapestry pulled thread by thread. We become wanderers in the vast desert of sin, our footprints disappearing in the shifting sands behind us. Like sheep who have strayed from their shepherd's watch, we find ourselves exposed and vulnerable when darkness descends, with no refuge from the prowling shadows of doubt and despair.

As creatures formed for divine connection, this spiritual displacement leaves us adrift in a fog of uncertainty, haunted by an inexplicable emptiness that no earthly pleasure can fill. In this hollow space between who we were and who we've become, we're forced to confront the ghost of our former selves.

The soul finally awakens from its slumber in this crucible of crisis. Like a compass needle swimming back to true north, something deep within us awakens to the staggering distance we've wandered from our authentic path. This awakening sparks a primal yearning to reclaim our divine heritage, to trace our way back to the source of our being.

Yet some souls remain perpetual wanderers, spending lifetimes circling the edges of this awakening without ever taking that first brave step toward home—spiritual nomads forever searching for an anchor they cannot name.

## Conceptualizing the Awakening—The Prodigal Son

I find myself repeatedly revisiting the parable of the Prodigal Son, like a well-trod path to a sacred spring. In its ancient lines, I discover fresh revelations of God's boundless mercy—a love so vast it stretches beyond the horizons of our worst transgressions. Even when we've dissolved ourselves in sin's acid rain, even when we imagine divine fury must surely await us, this story whispers of a different truth.

We must view this parable through the perspective of its original telling to fully understand its revolutionary nature. Here, in this masterpiece of divine storytelling, Jesus paints a portrait of God that shatters our preconceptions—not a stern judge waiting to condemn, but a father scanning the horizon with tear-filled eyes, waiting for the first glimpse of his child's return. Our true identity, like an inheritance that can never be squandered, remains safely held in His house, waiting for our homecoming.

The story emerged from a moment of criticism, when the Pharisees' accusations hung bitter in the air: "This man welcomes sinners and eats with them..." (Luke 15:2). In response, Jesus unfurled this tapestry of grace, weaving together the tale of a father and his two sons—a story that would echo through centuries, offering hope to every lost child seeking their way home.

## THE BOY FROM BRAZIL

The tale unfolds with the younger son's brazen demand—a request that essentially wished his father dead—as he claimed his inheritance and ventured into the wilderness of his own desires. Like autumn leaves scattered by a harsh wind, his wealth disappeared, and with it, the fair-weather friends who had flocked to his temporary abundance. The Jewish son, a prince of his father's household, found himself envious of the swine he fed in a pigpen. It was here, in this lowest of valleys, that dawn finally broke in his darkened soul.

His awakening came as a whispered revelation: "How many of my father's hired servants have food to spare, and here I am starving to death!" (Luke 15:17, NIV). In that moment of clarity, sharp as breaking glass, the fog of his rebellion lifted. Though he had tried to bury his identity beneath layers of sin and self-will, his true nature—that of a beloved son—rose like a phoenix from the ashes of his squandered life. His soul, long muffled by the world's empty promises, finally cried out for its true home.

But it's in the father's response that this parable blazes with divine light. Where the son expected judgment, he found jubilation. Where he anticipated rejection, he discovered celebration. The father's running embrace—shocking for a dignified Eastern patriarch—the pristine robe covering his filth, the ring restoring his authority, the shoes dignifying his bare feet: each gift a symbol of restoration more complete than the son dared to imagine. Yet this radiant moment of grace cast a shadow: the older brother, outwardly faithful but inwardly bitter, stood in the darkness outside the celebration, his heart hardened by the very mercy that should have softened it.

In this masterful stroke, Jesus holds up a mirror to the Pharisees' souls. Like the elder brother, they stood in the courtyard of God's house, yet their hearts wandered far from His heart of mercy. Their physical proximity to the Father became their spiritual liability, their ceremonial cleanliness masking an interior drought of genuine love. Though they dwelt in the shadow of the temple, they had never truly dwelt in the warmth of divine grace.

The prodigal son, in contrast, embodied the paradox of spiritual strength through surrender. In the alchemy of his humility, his brokenness became the vessel for grace. Through his story, Jesus illuminates a profound truth: what matters most is not the outward performance of faith, but the inner yearning to know and be known by the Father. It's not about perfect attendance in the house, but about perfect abandonment to the heart of God. Faith divorced from this quest for true identity becomes mere ritual—a hollow shell of religion without relationship. We must anchor ourselves daily in the bedrock of who we are in Him, just as a tree must bury its roots deep to withstand life's challenges.

## Immigration

My own prodigal journey began on foreign soil, in the concrete canyons of Newark, New Jersey. It was 1989, and at nine years old, I found myself transplanted from the warm embrace of Brazil into the stark reality of American life. Like a seedling uprooted from familiar soil, I struggled to find purchase in this new terrain. Each day brought fresh reminders that I too was now a stranger in a strange land, echoing the ancient stories of God's people in exile.

America became the crucible of my identity crisis. Each passing day stripped away another layer of who I thought I was, like paint peeling from an old wall. The familiar rhythms of Brazilian life gave way to an alien choreography I couldn't master. The language barrier arose like an invisible wall, turning me into a silent observer in a world of fast-paced English. In this new landscape, dignity seemed a luxury not

## THE BOY FROM BRAZIL

afforded to immigrants like me—we were shadows moving through the margins of American life. Oh, if only I had understood then what revelation has since taught me: that all Christians walk this earth as spiritual immigrants, temporary residents whose true citizenship lies in a kingdom beyond borders. But in those early days, I was simply a lost child in a maze of concrete and steel, my heart yearning for a home I could no longer define.

In the void of my solitude, my mind transformed into a reverberating chamber of uncertainty and longing. The voices that filled this emptiness were persistent companions, whispering questions about my worth, my place, and my future. Like a house of mirrors, each reflection showed a different version of who I might become, yet none seemed to capture the truth of who I was meant to be. This internal cacophony, born from the fertile soil of displacement, became the siren song that would lead me further from my true path. The foreign land's challenges weren't just external obstacles to overcome—they became the architects of my internal exile.

Desperate to outrun my own shadow of inadequacy, I began a frantic chase after mirages in the desert of my displacement. Like a drowning man clutching at anything that floats, I reached for relationship after relationship, seeking shelter in the arms of strangers. Each new romance promised salvation from my loneliness, yet each proved to be another temporary oasis—appearing solid from a distance but dissolving into sand at my touch. These connections, born from desperation rather than genuine intimacy, became a carousel of empty embraces, spinning faster and faster as I sought the one thing that always seemed just out of reach: belonging.

This desperate dance of belonging drove me deeper into materialism's glittering embrace. In a culture where worth was measured in possessions, I adorned myself with the trappings of success like a peacock preening its feathers. Each designer label, each luxury purchase, became another layer of armor against my perceived inadequacy. Like a Venus flytrap's deceptive beauty, I cultivated an attractive exterior that lured others close while masking the emptiness within. The attention I received became my drug of choice, and I found myself willing to pay any price—moral, spiritual, or financial—to maintain this carefully constructed façade. With each compromise, I sank deeper into the quicksand of sin, watching helplessly as both my cultural heritage and spiritual birthright slipped through my fingers like grains of sand. I had exchanged the authentic garments of my identity for knock-off vestments of a life that stood in stark opposition to God's Kingdom.

Now, when I look back through the lens of grace at those first disorienting days in America, I see the prodigal son's story written in the ink of my own tears. Many read his tale with judgment, assuming his request for inheritance came with a premeditated plan for debauchery. We portray him as a calculated rebel, his heart already hardened to the path of destruction he would embark on. But standing in the shoes of an immigrant, a stranger in a strange land, I recognize a more nuanced truth.

Through the prism of my own exile, I see in this young man not a willful rebel, but a lost soul caught in the undertow of displacement. His descent into excess wasn't plotted on some moral map—it was the desperate flailing of someone trying to find solid ground in shifting sands. Like me, he discovered that identity, when not firmly anchored in divine truth, becomes as fluid as mercury, taking the shape of whatever vessel the world provides. Both of us felt like seedlings torn from familiar soil, our roots exposed to harsh elements, bending in the direction of the winds of acceptance.

## Living in Sin

For three decades, I wandered through a spiritual wasteland of my own making, a desert where mirages of pleasure masked the oases of true peace. Sin became both my compass and my chains, leading me further into darkness while binding me to its hollow promises. I was like a ship with a broken rudder, drifting aimlessly on seas of desire, mistaking the storm for the harbor. Faith and relationship with God were foreign languages I couldn't comprehend, their syllables lost in the cacophony of worldly pursuits. I had become a vessel meant for living water, instead filled with the brackish waters of temporal satisfaction.

My body became my betraying compass, its hungers and impulses drowning out the whispered wisdom of Proverbs 5-6. Like a moth drawn repeatedly to destroying flames, I fluttered from one relationship to another, mistaking the burn of passion for the warmth of love. Each new connection held the promise of paradise but instead delivered purgatory, and due to my spiritual blindness, I failed to recognize how each relationship further deteriorated my soul. I was too intoxicated by temporal pleasure to recognize the spiritual gangrene setting in, too busy chasing shadows to notice I was running from the light.

In the first chapter of Romans, Paul unveils a haunting truth about humanity's spiritual descent—a mirror in which I saw my own fall reflected with startling clarity. He reveals that the fingerprints of God are pressed into every sunset, written in every star, whispered in every breath of wind. Creation itself testifies to its Creator, leaving us without excuse. Yet when we turn from this divine evidence to craft deities of our own design—whether carved from wood or fashioned from our desires—we set in motion a spiritual entropy that leads to our undoing. His words echo with prophetic power:

*28. And since they did not see fit to acknowledge God, God gave them up to a debased mind to do what ought not to be done. 29. They were filled with all manner of unrighteousness, evil, covetousness, and malice. They are full of envy, murder, strife, deceit, and maliciousness. They are gossips. 30. slanderers, haters of God, insolent, haughty, boastful, inventors of evil, disobedient to parents, 31. foolish, faithless, heartless, ruthless. 32. Though they know God's righteous decree that those who practice such things deserve to die, they not only do them but approve of those who practice them"* (Romans 1:20-31).

The progression is as inevitable as water flowing downhill—a spiritual law as certain as gravity. Turn from the living God, and the vacuum will be filled with dead idols. Like a garden left untended, the soul becomes overrun with thorns of depravity. This was the prodigal son's descent, and it became mine. In the strange soil of a new land, we both found ourselves unable—or perhaps unwilling—to recognize the God who had followed us there. The golden calves of pleasure and status filled our vision until we could see nothing else.

Psalm 91 had promised shelter beneath the wings of the Almighty, a fortress of divine protection and peace. However, I opted to construct my own shelter using the fragile materials of worldly success, creating an impressive structure that could not endure even the slightest spiritual disturbance. I became an architect of my own destruction, blueprint in hand, convinced that my design for happiness would prove superior to God's.

In my spiritual myopia, I had relegated the Creator of galaxies to a footnote in my self-authored story. My relationship with Him became as superficial as morning mist, evaporating in the heat of my own desires. I fashioned a designer deity—a god made in my image, one

THE BOY FROM BRAZIL                    147

who would bend to my will rather than transform my heart. Like a child playing with a compass made of paper, I spun directionless in the moral wilderness, mistaking motion for progress. Yet divine mercy writes straight with crooked lines. Like the prodigal son before me, I found myself at the precipice of spiritual bankruptcy, where the thin thread of grace connecting me to my Creator had stretched gossamer-fine, threatening to snap under the weight of my rebellion. But even there, in that midnight hour of the soul, God's hand stayed the scissors of judgment. Instead of delivering me to the full harvest of my sinful seeds—the "giving over" that Paul warns of in Romans 1:26—He preserved that fragile lifeline. In the pig pen of my own making, consciousness dawned like a desert sunrise. My soul, long muted by the world's cacophony, finally found its voice, whispering ancient truths: You have wandered far. The journey home will be long. But every step toward the Father, no matter how painful, carries the promise of restoration.

## A Realization

The awakening came not as a thunderbolt but as a slow-dawning realization, like morning light seeping through drawn curtains. The glittering prizes I had pursued turned out to be worthless, transforming into dust in my grasp. All my worldly pursuits had left me hollow, each achievement ringing as empty as a bronze gong in an abandoned temple. Through the fog of my disillusionment, I caught glimpses of my spiritual siblings—those who had found shelter in the Father's embrace—their lives radiating a contentment that my carefully curated existence had never known. After three decades of spiritual exile, my soul stirred with a forgotten hunger, recognizing at last its true sustenance. Like a compass needle spinning through chaos before finding true north, my heart oriented itself toward God, sensing in Him the peace that had eluded me in all my wanderings. Though shame whispered that I had forfeited my right to sonship, something deeper—perhaps grace itself—beckoned me toward home.

Doubt stalked my first tentative steps toward redemption, its shadow long and dark across my path. The ledger of my transgressions appeared to be inscribed in permanent ink, each page bearing the weight of years spent in rebellion. Yet as I approached the throne of grace, trembling like a storm-battered sparrow, I began to glimpse the vast ocean of divine mercy—deeper than my deepest sin, wider than my widest wandering. My finite understanding of forgiveness shattered against the infinite expanse of God's grace.

Then came the story that would break open my understanding of divine mercy—Dismas, the thief on the cross. Here was a man whose life had been a tapestry of darkness, whose hands had wrought misery until the very hour of his execution. Yet in his final moments, suspended between heaven and earth beside the Son of God, he found redemption in a whispered plea: "Remember me." His story crashed through my carefully constructed barriers of unworthiness like a battering ram. If paradise could open its gates to a lifetime criminal in his eleventh hour, surely there was hope for me. Like Dismas, I too needed only to be remembered. Like him, I discovered that it's never too late to choose a different ending to your story. And like the prodigal son before us both, I finally understood that my Father's arms had never stopped reaching for me, even when I had stopped reaching for Him.

## The Prodigal Son Phenomenon: The New Identity

This metamorphosis of the soul—this radical reorientation of identity—is what I've come to call the prodigal son phenomenon. It's a

# THE BOY FROM BRAZIL

spiritual awakening that begins not with external voices but with an internal revelation. The prodigal's transformation hinged not on what others whispered about him in the village square, but on the moment he dared to reimagine his own story. "It's not what people are saying about you that gets in the way," the wisdom echoes, "it's what you're saying about yourself, what you're saying about your life, what you're putting in the atmosphere." These words resonate deeply within my restored heart, reflecting my own journey from self-imposed exile to redemption. This memoir itself stands as a testament to that sacred moment when I finally rose from the pig pen of my past and dared to speak a new truth into existence. For in God's economy of grace, it's never the opening chapter that defines us—it's the courage to allow Him to write a different ending.

In the gallery of divine grace, another portrait hangs beside the prodigal's—a tale of two sons that illuminates the paradox of redemption with stark clarity:

*"28. What do you think? A man had two sons. And he went to the first and said, 'Son, go and work in the vineyard today.' 29. And he answered, 'I will not,' but afterward he changed his mind and went. 30. And he went to the other son and said the same. And he answered, 'I go, sir,' but did not go. 31. Which of the two did the will of his father?" They said, "The first." Jesus said to them, "Truly, I say to you, the tax collectors and the prostitutes go into the kingdom of God before you. 32. For John came to you in the way of righteousness, and you did not believe him, but the tax collectors and the prostitutes believed him. And even when you saw it, you did not afterward change your minds and believe him"* (Matthew 21).

Here lies perhaps the most radical revelation of divine grace—a holy paradox that turns our human logic on its head. The son whose first word was "no" but whose final action was "yes" proved truer than the one whose lips spoke righteousness while his heart harbored rebellion. This parable brims with hope for every late-arriving laborer, every last-minute convert, and every prodigal making their way home through the encroaching dusk. In our Father's vineyard, the final chapter holds greater significance than all the preceding volumes put together. The prostitutes and tax collectors—society's designated outcasts—surge ahead into the kingdom not because of their past but because they recognized the dawn of grace when it broke across their darkness. They remind us that it's not the stumbling start that matters, but the direction of our final steps. For in our Father's vineyard, even those who arrive as the sun sets will find themselves welcomed as full heirs of the harvest.

## Sacred Sexuality

The first steps on my journey back to authentic identity required more than mere course correction—it demanded a complete rewiring of my understanding of sexuality and its sacred purpose. Ephesians 4:17-18 sliced through my confusion with precision:

"So I tell you this and insist on it in the Lord, that you must no longer live as the Gentiles do, in the futility of their thinking. They are darkened in their understanding and separated from the life of God because of the ignorance that is in them due to the hardening of their hearts."

These ancient words held up a mirror to my modern struggle, reflecting back the futility of a life lived in spiritual darkness.

My youth and curiosity had led me down paths that transformed sexuality—meant to be a sacred expression of divine love—into something profane and hollow. Like the prodigal son, I had squandered my spiritual inheritance in the brothels of modern life, trading the

# THE BOY FROM BRAZIL                    151

pearl of great price for cheap imitations of intimacy. Each encounter
left me spiritually poorer until I found myself in my own version
of the pigpen, feeding on relationships that could never nourish my
soul. However, similar to the prodigal's epiphany amidst the swine, my
awakening arrived following yet another fruitless encounter. The time
had come to reclaim my birthright as God's beloved son, to exchange
the rags of promiscuity for the robes of righteousness.

Standing now in the light of divine sonship, I've come to understand that holiness begins with radical honesty—first with ourselves,
then with God. Like a runner shedding heavy garments before a race,
I began stripping away the accumulated weight of my past transgressions. Hebrews 12:1 became my rallying cry: "Let us cast off everything
that hinders and the sin that so easily entangles, and let us run with
perseverance the race marked out for us." Each surrender lifted another
burden, and each confession broke another chain.

The first steps away from my old life were like emerging from a cave
into dawning light—painful at first, but gradually revealing a world
awash in colors I had forgotten existed. Peace settled over my soul
like morning dew, gentle but transformative. God's reception of me
mirrored the prodigal's homecoming, but with an intensity I hadn't
dared to hope for. He didn't just offer me a new robe—He gave me
a new identity, marked my heart with an indelible seal of belonging.
The Holy Spirit's fire became my internal compass, making the old
pleasures that once seemed so alluring now feel like ash in my mouth.

I often compare my escape from sexual sin to Lot's family's flight
from Sodom and Gomorrah, with divine mercy guiding us from
imminent destruction. Just as God set His mark of protection on
Lot's household, I felt His sovereign hand shielding me from the life
I was leaving behind. The warning to "remember Lot's wife" echoes
in my consciousness whenever temptation whispers of the past. Her

fate—frozen in a backward glance—serves as my deterrent against nostalgia for Egypt's fleshpots. I've tasted the bread of my Father's house; I can no longer stomach the husks that once seemed satisfying. The foreign land of sin has lost its allure, replaced by the incomparable comfort of dwelling in God's presence.

## Transformed into God's Image

Scripture's foundational truth echoes through the corridors of time: we bear the imprint of the divine, like ancient coins still showing traces of their royal stamp. Our identity is inextricably woven into the fabric of God's own nature—try to separate the two, and both unravel. Like a mirror that must be turned toward light to serve its purpose, we can only reflect His image when our lives are oriented toward His presence. My transformation required more than mere behavioral modification; it demanded a complete spiritual reorientation, a turning from shadow to substance.

My journey mirrored the prodigal's in its arc from falsity to authenticity, from hollow performance to genuine presence. Each step away from my counterfeit self was a step toward the person God had always intended me to be. Through this metamorphosis—this holy alchemy of grace—I began to glimpse the true magnitude of divine mercy. Like a master artist restoring a damaged masterpiece, God worked with infinite patience to reveal the original image beneath years of accumulated grime. His relentless pursuit of my soul bears witness to a love that is unwavering, akin to a shepherd who braves any wilderness to retrieve a lost sheep.

In this divine romance, I discovered that God's very name is Faithfulness, His nature written in the language of infinite patience. The words of 2 Peter 3:9 became not just scripture but personal testimony:

## THE BOY FROM BRAZIL

"The Lord is not slow in keeping his promise, as some understand slowness. Instead, he is patient with you, not wanting anyone to perish, but everyone to come to repentance." His timing, I learned, moves to the rhythm of redemption rather than the hurried pace of human expectations.

The tale of Israel resonates throughout history, a testament to God's boundless mercy. Again and again, His chosen people strayed; again and again, His love pursued them. Each cycle of rebellion and restoration wrote another chapter in love's persistent narrative. Like a master choreographer, He wove their stumbling steps into a dance of redemption, His discipline the gentle correction of a Father teaching His children to walk. From the golden calf to the glory of the cross, every divine intervention testified to a love that would stop at nothing—not even death—to bring His beloved home.

The contrast between our past and present becomes a testament to divine artistry—like a before-and-after portrait painted in the colors of grace. In this light, Saul's transformation from persecutor to apostle blazes with new significance in my understanding. Here was a man whose hands had been stained with martyrs' blood, whose breath had carried threats of death against the church, yet whose heart proved fertile soil for heaven's most dramatic renovation. The divine encounter on the Damascus road not only changed his direction but also completely rewrote his identity. The zealous Pharisee became the passionate apostle; the hunter of Christians transformed into Christianity's most ardent defender.

Now, like Paul before me, I feel the weight of my testimony as both gift and responsibility. My story of transformation becomes a lighthouse beacon for others still lost in similar storms. Having emerged from my chrysalis of sin, I bear witness to divine possibility—proof that no life is beyond the reach of God's transforming touch. Each scar in my past becomes a signpost of hope, each failure redeemed into a lesson that might spare others the long detour through darkness I once traveled. In sharing these chronicles of grace, I become part of an ancient tradition of transformed lives pointing others toward home—another voice in the eternal chorus testifying that no matter how far we've strayed, the Father's arms remain open, waiting to welcome us back to our true identity in Him.

The question of identity has become a fundamental issue in our modern society. Like tectonic plates shifting beneath our feet, conversations about identity—particularly within the context of the growing LGBTQ+ community—create tremors that ripple through families, churches, and communities. While recognizing the fundamental human dignity and civil rights of all people, we find ourselves navigating increasingly complex waters of personal and collective identity.

At the core of this discourse lies a profound question: To what extent is identity fixed or fluid? Like a river cutting through bedrock, this question carves through layers of biology, theology, and human experience. From a biblical perspective, our identity comes etched in the bedrock of creation itself—a divine blueprint written into our very DNA. This God-given identity stands as an anchor in the shifting seas of cultural opinion, a North Star by which to navigate the complex waters of self-discovery. Yet this truth must be spoken with both conviction and compassion, recognizing the deep waters of human struggle and pain that often surround questions of identity.

Just as mathematical truths provide immutable reference points—a circle remains distinct from a straight line regardless of perspective—and just as the wavelength of red light remains constant despite varying perceptions, certain aspects of identity are written into the fabric of creation itself. These foundational truths serve not as

# THE BOY FROM BRAZIL

weapons of judgment but as lighthouses of clarity in stormy cultural seas.

In this sea of shifting cultural narratives, the Bible stands as our fixed point of reference—an ancient yet ever-relevant compass pointing toward truth. Like a master architect's original blueprints, Scripture reveals the divine design for human identity. The words of Genesis 5:2 ring across millennia with crystalline clarity: "He created them male and female and blessed them. And he named them 'Mankind' when they were created." This foundational truth emerges not as a mere biological observation but as a divine pronouncement woven into the very fabric of creation—each human life crafted with intentional purpose and blessed with inherent dignity.

When the anchors of identity are dislodged—whether by cultural currents, personal trauma, or societal pressure—the resulting crisis can feel like being set adrift on stormy seas. Modern psychiatry recognizes this phenomenon as an identity crisis: a profound period of disorientation where one's sense of self becomes unmoored from its foundations. Like a tree whose roots have lost their grip in shifting soil, individuals in such a crisis often struggle to find stable ground. While we acknowledge the powerful influence of community and culture in shaping our self-understanding, we must recognize that true identity exploration must ultimately lead us back to our Creator's original design.

The prophet Isaiah captures this tension with striking imagery: "Woe to those who quarrel with their Maker, those who are nothing but potsherds among the potsherds on the ground. Does the clay say to the potter, 'What are you making?' Does your work say, 'The potter has no hands'?" (Isaiah 45:9). These words paint a powerful picture of the relationship between Creator and created—not to diminish human dignity, but to illuminate the source of our true identity. Like a master potter whose hands know precisely the vessel they intend to shape, God's design for each life carries both purpose and beauty.

In this divine economy of identity, only the Master Artist holds the authority to define His masterpiece. Like a signature at the bottom of a priceless painting, His creative authority stands as the final word on who we truly are.

For those who have found their way to Christ's embrace, an even more profound transformation occurs. Our identity breaks free from the prison of past sins and cultural conditioning, emerging into the light of radical grace. No matter how dark our history—whether stained by the ink of a thousand transgressions or marked by years of rebellion—a supernatural metamorphosis awaits. The words of 2 Corinthians 5:17 burst forth like dawn after the longest night: "Therefore, if anyone is in Christ, the new creation has come: The old has gone, the new is here!"

This is not just a superficial alteration, nor merely a fresh start. This is resurrection itself—the dead heart finding its beat again in the rhythm of divine love. When we surrender to Christ as Lord and Savior, we discover our true names written not in the shifting sands of cultural identity but in the eternal bedrock of God's family record. We are adopted into royalty, grafted into the divine family tree, marked with an identity that neither time nor circumstance can erase: Beloved. Child of God. Heir of Grace. This is who we are. This is who we were always meant to be.

## Points for Reflection

1. "Describe a significant moment or experience in your life that led you to your faith journey. What changes did you notice in yourself before and after this turning point?"

# THE BOY FROM BRAZIL                    157

2. "If you were having a conversation with someone unfamiliar with faith concepts, how would you explain God's grace using everyday examples or personal experiences?"

3. "We all face moments of regret or guilt in our lives. Can you share a time when you struggled with these feelings and how your faith helped you find peace or resolution?"

# Chapter 8

---

# Full Circle

*"For I know the plans I have for you," declares the LORD, "plans to
prosper you and not to harm you, plans to give you hope and a future."*
*Jeremiah 29:11*

*"When you are at the top, be careful of the monster called PRIDE
Pride will make you look down on the people who haven't attained your
level of success.
When you are at the bottom, be careful of the monster called BITTER-
NESS
Bitterness will make you jealous and think that other people are the
reason you haven't made it.
When you are on the way to the top, be careful of the monster called
GREED
Greed will make you impatient and make you steal or
seek shortcuts.
When you are on your way down, be careful of the
monster called DESPAIR
Despair will make you think it's all over yet there
is still hope."*

THE BOY FROM BRAZIL                    159

*- Nelson Mandela*


## Lavender Grace

Crowned in lavender silk and summer light,
She dissolves into sacred serenity—
Where divine glory spills through leaves
Like molten gold through stained glass.


In this cathedral of open sky,
Heaven's whispers brush her skin
Like wind through prayer flags.


Butterflies rise like painted prayers—
Each wing a psalm,
Each flight a blessing,
Each breath a hallelujah.


They dance on currents of grace,
Blessing flowers with gossamer kisses,
Carrying secrets between earth and sky—


These messengers of joy who lead us
To where light and spirit intertwine,
Where every breath reveals the miracle
Of being wondrously, radiantly alive.

## Graça Lavanda

Coroada em seda lavanda e luz de verão,
Ela se dissolve em sagrada serenidade—
Onde a glória divina derrama-se através das folhas
Como ouro derretido através do vitral.

Nesta catedral de céu aberto,
Os sussurros do céu roçam sua pele
Como vento através de bandeiras de oração.

Borboletas se elevam como preces pintadas—
Cada asa um salmo,
Cada voo uma bênção,
Cada respiro um aleluia.

Elas dançam em correntes de graça,
Abençoando flores com beijos de seda,
Carregando segredos entre terra e céu—

Estes mensageiros de alegria que nos guiam
Até onde luz e espírito se entrelaçam,
Onde cada respiração revela o milagre
De estar maravillosamente, radiantemente viva.

The taste of mango still haunts me—sweet, sticky nectar that drips with memories of a life left behind. Like Dorothy before her cyclone, I too lived in a world of vibrant color, though mine wasn't Kansas but Brazil. The sugarcane juice vendors would press the stalks until they wept their cold, sweet tears into plastic cups, and I knew their

## THE BOY FROM BRAZIL                    161

taste as intimately as I knew my own heartbeat. The endless Sundays
stretched like taffy, melting into the lake, and sun-drenched afternoons dissolved into laughter shared with my best friend Jacqueline.
Together, we traced the veins of Belo Horizonte's streets, our footsteps
echoing against ancient cobblestones as we mapped our kingdom with
the fearless curiosity of youth. Unlike the little girl from Kansas who
dreamed of a place far away over the rainbow, I was already dancing
beneath my own rainbow's embrace, living my best life in my own little
corner, in my own little place.

But storms have a way of brewing when skies seem clearest, and
my tornado came not in swirling clouds but in airplane tickets and
visa stamps, hurling me across hemispheres to land with a thunderous
crash in Newark, New Jersey—a gray city that seemed to have forgotten the meaning of color. Living there felt like learning to breathe un-
derwater—every word a bubble that burst before reaching the surface,
every face a distorted reflection in turbulent seas. It forced a complete
adjustment, like a butterfly struggling against the chrysalis, wings still
wet with metamorphosis. From the moment I set foot in that concrete
jungle in 1989, homesickness enveloped me, and the American Dream
metamorphosed into a personal journey that I hoped would somehow
guide me back to my true self.

In place of ruby slippers, destiny handed me something far more
powerful—the leather-bound Book of Truth, its pages worn smooth
from desperate midnight readings. It became my compass, my shield,
my sword. Like David facing his Goliaths, I encountered towering adversaries along my path—not wicked witches, but demons dressed in
modern cloth: identity crisis lurking like a shadow, addiction whispering sweet poisons, and lust laying velvet traps. I'm not saying I would
have handled these things differently back home in Brazil, but at least
there, the battlefield would have been familiar ground; the air would

have tasted of home. America was an alien landscape where even the stars seemed to speak a foreign tongue, and I was left scrambling to decipher its cryptic message while dodging its spiritual arrows.

Like Moses' people before me, I found myself wandering in my own wilderness—a barren expanse of soul-searching where minutes stretched into years. My tears watered that desert soil; my complaints echoed off invisible walls. Like Lot's wife, I couldn't help but look back, my gaze drawn to the shimmer of what-ifs and might-have-beens, each memory a mirage that threatened to turn me to salt. God never intended for me to be there. I had stumbled into a carnival of false promises, where neon-lit tempters played shell games with my soul and masked charlatans dealt in counterfeit dreams. This was a place where I was not focused on Jesus, a glittering waystation on the road to somewhere real. Just as a butterfly has to find nectar to live, I had to seek the sweet sustenance of Faith, following my yellow brick road not toward an emerald mirage but toward the genuine glory of my true home.

## Recognizing the Enemy

Like a warrior awakening to the true nature of his battlefield, I finally saw my enemy's face in the mirror of truth—not flesh and blood, but principalities of darkness wearing familiar masks. Ephesians 6:11 became my battle cry, each piece of God's armor clicking into place like divine puzzle pieces: "Put on the whole armor of God, that ye may be able to stand against the wiles of the devil." This wasn't merely culture shock or homesickness—this was spiritual warfare, with every step forward contested by shadows. The enemy's arrows came disguised as doubts, his artillery masked as anxiety, but through the smoke of each battle, I glimpsed my Father's shield above me. The devil, that ancient serpent, struck again and again, but his fangs found only faith's armor, and his lies shattered against truth's bedrock.

Like Dorothy collecting her unlikely companions, I gathered friends along my journey—some as steady as the Tin Man, others as courageous as the Lion. Their presence blessed me like rain in desert places, their laughter a shelter in storms. Yet even as I celebrated their victories, something gnawed at my heart—a hunger no earthly feast could satisfy, a thirst no worldly well could quench.

I always felt this longing to go home and to be closer to my heavenly father. Ecclesiastes 3:11 whispered its ancient wisdom: "He has made everything beautiful in its time. Also, he has put eternity into man's heart..." Like a cosmic homing beacon embedded in our souls, this eternal longing pulses in every human heart. Even while we are out in the world, that divine frequency keeps calling us homeward, a melody only our spirit can hear. God placed eternity in the hearts of man.

## A Teaching Moment

Sometimes, the most ordinary moments conceal truth like a pearl hidden from view. One such pearl emerged from a stranger's testimony, gleaned from the fluorescent-lit aisles of a late-night grocery store. There, amid the weary shuffling of shopping carts and the mechanical beep of scanners, stood a family tableau: a mother and her two sons—one hovering on the cusp of adolescence, the other barely steady on his feet. The younger one's wails pierced the tired air, his small finger pointing insistently at the treasure his brother held: a package of glowsticks.

Peace arrived in the form of a single glowstick, placed in tiny hands by a mother's grace. Joy bloomed like a sudden sunrise on the toddler's face as he paraded his prize through the checkout line, leaving trails of innocent laughter in his wake. But then—that moment when joy seemed stolen, when his brother's hands reclaimed the treasure. Before maternal intervention could unfold, before tears could fully form, something magical happened: a snap, a bend, and suddenly darkness transformed into light. The older brother's words fell like prophecy in that fluorescent temple: "I had to break it to get its full effect."

In that ordinary moment, heaven's whisper became a thunderclap in my soul. God's voice echoed through that simple truth: "My child, like that glowstick, your breaking wasn't your ending—it was your illumination. Each crack in your heart, each fracture in your plans, each shatter in your expectations—these were not mere wounds, but fissures through which My light could finally shine. Your yellow brick road, with all its twists and tumbles, was never just a path of trials—it was your transformation trail."

Each of us carries a divine fingerprint, unique and irreplaceable in the vast tapestry of existence. Yes, the path stretches long and thorny before us, each step an exercise in perseverance. In those moments when surrender seems sweetest, remember: you are not a cosmic accident, but a carefully crafted miracle. Your presence here ripples through the universe in ways you cannot fathom. Like a chrysalis in winter, your darkness is not your destiny—it's your transformation chamber, where wings of purpose unfold in sacred silence.

The true tragedy isn't in the falling—we all fall, like autumn leaves caught in life's whirlwind. No, the real tragedy lies in remaining face-down in the dust when wings were made for soaring. Proverbs 24:15 rings like a battle cry across centuries: "For though a righteous man falls seven times, he rises again..." Each fall is not a failure but a foundation, each stumble not an ending but a beginning. Rise, warrior-child of God, for divine hands steady your shoulders. Your storm wasn't your destruction—it was your dedication ceremony.

# THE BOY FROM BRAZIL                                                165

Like Dorothy's ruby slippers, your power has been with you since
the beginning, humming quietly beneath your doubts, waiting to be
recognized. Your past? It's a chapter, not the whole story. Let it be
your teacher, not your jailer. In this world of shadows and sirens,
let your compass be the dreams God planted in your heart like stars.
Your heavenly Father didn't craft you for limitation—He designed you
for liberation. When this truth finally penetrates your soul's bedrock,
transformation becomes not just possible, but inevitable.

Philippians whispers an ancient remedy for modern chaos: surrender your anxiety at heaven's threshold, wrap your prayers in gratitude's
golden paper, and lay them at your Father's feet. Then watch as divine peace—not the world's fragile cease-fire, but God's unshakeable
shalom—descends like morning dew, wrapping your heart and mind
in a fortress of tranquility. This is the alchemy of alignment: when
your spirit finds its true North in Him, chaos transforms into choreography, and confusion dissolves into sacred certainty.

## My Yellow Brick Road

Three decades and one year—a lifetime measured in seasons away
from Belo Horizonte, my personal Emerald City. Time hasn't dimmed
its colors in my mind; if anything, memory has polished each cobblestone until it gleams like jewels in my heart's treasury. Every remembered street corner shimmers with possibility; each recalled sunset
burns more golden than the last. When the whisper came that it was
time to return, it resonated through my bones like a bell's clear tone—a
calling to excavate those precious memories from the chambers of
dreams where they'd been carefully preserved.

Like Dorothy needed her companions on the yellow brick road, my
journey home required its own guardian angel—Jaqueline, my child-

hood confidante, and her family. God's provision often comes wearing familiar faces, and her February phone call became my burning bush moment, a divine appointment disguised as casual conversation. Those five-hour calls became my sanctuary, where laughter and tears mingled like rain and sunshine, creating rainbows of healing. I was a battle-weary warrior, and she became God's chosen medic, applying balm to old wounds with each shared memory.

She remained unchanged in essence—still that ethereal figure in her lavender hat, dancing through memory's garden while butterflies traced sacred geometries around her. When I finally touched down on Brazilian soil, I wore my exile's uniform: a threadbare shirt and worn-out Adidas, symbols of my long wandering. But like a snake shedding its old skin, I was ready to clothe myself in new garments, both literal and metaphorical. Each new purchase became a declaration of rebirth, a tangible sign of internal transformation.

Standing there, I watched as life unfurled before me like a pristine canvas, each moment a new brushstroke in God's masterpiece. Colors I had forgotten existed blazed across my vision—the burnt orange of Brazilian sunsets, the emerald depths of mountain valleys, the sapphire sparkle of childhood memories restored. Every breath painted new life into old dreams; every heartbeat added depth to the divine artwork of homecoming. This wasn't just a return; it was a resurrection.

Throughout these pages, butterflies dance not merely as delicate insects but as living parables of transformation. Their presence in my narrative isn't mere coincidence or literary flourish—they are the perfect metaphor for my journey's essence. Like these winged prophets of change, my life has been a sequence of metamorphoses, each stage necessary, each struggle sacred. But this return to Brazilian soil, this reunion with Jaqueline and her family—this was my final emergence, my ultimate transformation. From the chrysalis of exile, I emerged not

# THE BOY FROM BRAZIL

just changed but transfigured, my wings finally dried and ready for flight in the sunshine of God's grace.

When you whisper the word "church," what images ripple through your consciousness? Perhaps your mind conjures stained glass throwing rainbow shadows across wooden pews, or the familiar harmony of hymns rising like incense to vaulted ceilings. In your childhood memories, maybe it stands as a solid structure punctuating Sunday mornings with its bell's clear call. While dictionaries may reduce it to a mere "building for public Christian worship," the truth lies deeper, akin to roots beneath sacred soil.

Peter's confession, crafted not by human wisdom but by divine insight, resonated through time in that sacred moment. This truth declaration became more than mere words; it transformed into the cornerstone upon which Christ would build His living temple. Here was the blueprint for a church not made of stone and mortar, but of flesh and spirit—an invincible fortress of faith that would stand unmoved against the gathering storms of darkness. When Jesus and Paul spoke of "church," they weren't describing architecture but a breathing, moving body of believers, each one a living stone in God's magnificent design.

The call to church isn't merely an invitation to Sunday service—it's a summons to belonging, a divine recognition that faith flourishes in community. Christ, in His infinite wisdom, knew the human heart's tendency to wither in isolation. Think of your own journey: haven't there been moments when your faith felt like a flickering flame in a storm? We've all walked through those valleys of doubt, those desert stretches where our spirits grow parched and weary. In our human frailty, we sometimes stumble, and the weight of our missteps can feel like chains dragging us down into shadows of shame.

This is precisely why James 5:16 offers us a lifeline of hope: "Therefore confess your sins to each other and pray for each other so that you may be healed." These words depict the flow of supernatural healing through the channels of human connection. Like a mighty river finding its path through multiple tributaries, the power of prayer multiplies when shared. Even those we might consider spiritual giants—our most reverent pastors and ministers—need this sacred connection, this holy vulnerability.

In the modern church, we've given this ancient practice a new name: accountability. But this isn't mere supervision—it's a sacred covenant between souls. An accountability partner becomes your spiritual mirror, reflecting both your progress and your blind spots with loving clarity. The crucial element here is permission—that deliberate opening of your heart's doors to another's careful scrutiny. Take a moment to reflect: how many people have you trusted with the keys to your inner sanctuary? If your answer is "none," consider this your divine invitation to seek such a relationship. Like a tree needs deep roots to reach toward heaven, your faith needs these anchoring connections to grow strong.

Where do we find these sacred mirrors of accountability? The answer lies within the living walls of the church itself. Like precious gems hidden in common earth, true friends—those rare souls who reflect God's love back to us—often sparkle brightest within the fellowship of believers. Yet many of us stumble through life's marketplace, searching for friendship in glittering bazaars of superficial connection, while overlooking the treasure vault in our spiritual home.

True friendship transcends the casual connections of our digital age. These divine appointments are forged in the furnace of shared faith, tempered by time and trial. They are the ones who guard your soul during turbulent times, embrace your triumphs as their own, and

# THE BOY FROM BRAZIL

speak truth when you've lost your path. Like Jonathan to David, they recognize God's anointing on your life and protect it fiercely.

Most precious of all, authentic spiritual friends never entice you toward the world's dimming lights. Instead, they are like celestial navigators, always pointing toward the North Star of Christ. Their presence in your life becomes a holy magnetism, drawing you ever closer to the divine presence. These are the friends who don't merely walk beside you—they walk with you toward eternity.

## Points for Reflection

1. "Who are your trusted confidants—the people you can be completely honest with about your spiritual journey, doubts, and struggles? How did you develop that level of trust with them?"

2. "What does authentic spiritual community mean to you? How has being part of a faith community shaped your growth, and what qualities do you look for in a supportive spiritual family?"

3. "Think of someone in your life who might be searching for spiritual meaning. What compassionate ways could you share your faith journey with them while respecting where they are in their own journey?"

# Chapter 9

---

# Closing Reflections

## Living Victoriously

*"Life is a journey with problems to solve and lessons to learn, but most of all, experiences to enjoy."*
*Unknown Author*

Like delicate threads woven into an infinite tapestry, our lives intersect and diverge in countless ways. Perhaps you see echoes of your own journey in my story, or perhaps your path has led you through entirely different valleys and peaks. Yet there is profound beauty in this diversity, for each life writes its own irreplaceable narrative upon the pages of time.

Just as no two snowflakes share the same crystalline pattern, no two human beings—not even identical twins—share the same fingerprints. These unique spirals and whorls etched into our skin serve as nature's signature, a testament to our individual distinctness. Like an

# THE BOY FROM BRAZIL

artist who never repeats the same brushstroke twice, the Creator has marked each of us with an unrepeatable design.

In the quiet whispers of Psalm 139, we find this truth echoed through the ages: "For you created my inmost being; you knit me together in my mother's womb. I praise you because I am fearfully and wonderfully made; your works are wonderful; I know that full well." These ancient words resonate with a timeless power, speaking to the sacred artistry behind our creation.

Within these sacred verses lies a profound truth: we are not mere accidents of creation but carefully crafted masterpieces. Ephesians 2:10 paints us as divine artwork, each soul a canvas touched by the Master's hand. Whether you drew your first breath in a gleaming hospital or a humble village, whether your childhood was filled with laughter or tears, you remain an irreplaceable masterpiece in the Creator's gallery. Every line of your story, every shade of your experience, bears His signature.

How futile, then, to measure ourselves against others—like comparing a sunset to a mountain stream, each beautiful in its own right. When we fall into the trap of comparison, we plant seeds of discontent that grow into thorny vines of anxiety and self-doubt. These poisonous tendrils of envy can strangle our joy, transform into bitter fruits of anger, and leave us feeling hollow and inadequate. The garden of our soul was never meant to harbor such destructive growth.

Life unfolds in seasons, each with its own timing and purpose. While others may seem to bask in perpetual summer, perhaps you're weathering a winter of waiting. But take heart—your spring will come. Consider God's timing as a never-ending feast: there's no need for haste or anxiety over portions when the abundance is boundless. Just as a garden doesn't bloom all at once, but in perfect succession, each flower opening in its appointed time, so too will your blessings unfold.

The wellspring of divine abundance runs deeper than the ocean's depths, wider than the cosmos itself. Your boldest prayers, your grandest dreams—they cannot exhaust the infinite resources of the Creator. Like stars scattered across the night sky, His blessings stretch beyond our ability to count them.

## Looking at the Big Picture: The Canvas of Life's Challenges

Life stretches before us like a vast canvas, painted not only in gentle strokes of joy but also in bold brushstrokes of adversity. As surely as rivers flow to the sea, trials and tribulations wind their way through our journey. Some challenges arise from the ripples of our own choices, others from the stones cast by those around us. The ancient wisdom of scripture whispers this truth across centuries: "In this world, you will have troubles of many kinds." These words don't merely warn—they prepare us for the intricate tapestry of human experience, where both light and shadow play essential roles in creating depth and meaning.

In our darkest hours, we often kneel before God, pleading for Him to chisel away our mountain-sized troubles. Yet perhaps the greater miracle lies not in the removal of our obstacles, but in the strengthening of our spirit to scale them. When faced with towering challenges, let us pray not just for lighter burdens, but for stronger shoulders—not for smoother paths, but for more resilient feet to walk them.

Who hasn't yearned for a life unmarred by difficulties? Yet consider this: just as muscles atrophy without resistance, so too might our spirit wither without challenge. Picture a butterfly emerging from its chrysalis—if we were to "help" by cutting away its confining cocoon,

# THE BOY FROM BRAZIL

we would rob it of the very struggle that strengthens its wings for flight. Like a master teacher who knows when to increase the complexity of lessons, life presents us with increasingly sophisticated challenges that shape us into stronger, wiser beings. An existence without obstacles would be as limiting as asking a university scholar to never progress beyond simple addition.

Like a double-edged sword, our challenges cut both ways—they can wound or strengthen, defeat or empower. When troubles first descend like storm clouds on our horizon, we often stand paralyzed, feeling as fragile as autumn leaves in a gale. These moments of crisis can feel like waves threatening to overwhelm us, pulling us into depths we never thought we'd face. However, every obstacle we conquer adds another strand to our resilience. Through this crucible of difficulty, we learn perhaps life's most profound lesson: that true strength often comes not from controlling our circumstances, but from surrendering to a power greater than ourselves. In acknowledging our limitations, we discover the limitless nature of divine guidance. This journey from self-reliance to divine dependence may be as challenging as scaling a mountain—each step requiring both courage and humility.

A daughter is telling her mother how everything is going wrong; she's failing algebra, her boyfriend broke up with her, and her best friend is moving away. As she listens, her mother is baking a cake and asks her daughter if she would like a snack. The daughter says, "Absolutely, Mom, I love your cake."

Picture a scene in a warm kitchen, where wisdom is about to be served alongside something sweet. A young girl sits at the counter, her world seemingly crumbling around her—algebra formulas dance mockingly in her mind, while the twin griefs of lost love and friendship cast shadows across her heart. Her mother, wise in the way that moms often are, moves purposefully through her baking ritual, each motion a step in an unfolding lesson.

"Would you like something special?" The mother asks, her hands dusted with flour, her eyes twinkling with knowing purpose. The daughter brightens momentarily; her love for her mother's baking is a small light in her darkness.

But then comes the unexpected: a bottle of cooking oil, offered like a strange gift. The daughter recoils. Raw eggs appear next, their pale shells gleaming with possibility—and potential disgust. One by one, the mother presents the isolated ingredients: flour, fine as desert sand; baking soda, bitter and plain. Each offer meets with increasing bewilderment and rejection.

The mother's eyes soften as she watches understanding begin to dawn on her daughter's face. "Each of these ingredients alone seems bitter, unpalatable, even worthless," she says, her hands moving to gather them together. "But in the Master Baker's hands, when mixed in perfect measure and transformed by the heat of His timing—" she gestures to the golden cake cooling on the rack, its sweet aroma filling the kitchen—"they "become something beautiful, something nourishing, something worth the wait."

Her voice gentles further, heavy with wisdom. "Life's hardships are like these raw ingredients, dear one. The failed test, the broken heart, the friend moving away—each feels bitter when tasted alone. But God, the Master Baker of our lives, sees the final recipe. He knows how to blend our trials and tears, our struggles and successes, into something more wonderful than we could imagine. We simply need to trust His timing, His measurements, and His divine heat of transformation."

The kitchen fills with holy silence as the truth of this simple lesson settles like sifted flour.

## THE BOY FROM BRAZIL

This kitchen wisdom echoes the ancient promise found in Romans 8:28: "And we know that in all things God works for the good of those who love him, who have been called according to his purpose." Like a master recipe passed down through generations, these words have comforted countless souls standing amid their own scattered ingredients of adversity.

Life unfolds like an epic journey, each step carved with purpose, each milestone etched with meaning. When the path grows steep and your spirit weary, whisper this truth to your anxious heart: "I may not be where I want to be, but I'm not where I used to be." Let gratitude be your compass—not just for the grand victories, but for the quiet triumphs, the small steps forward, and the moments of unexpected grace. When storms gather and threaten to eclipse your vision, shift your gaze from the looming clouds to the vast sky above. For in magnifying God rather than our difficulties, we discover that gratitude isn't just an attitude—it's the soil in which joy takes root and flourishes.

These ancient words from Thessalonians ring across centuries like a clear bell: "Give thanks in every circumstance, for this is God's will for you in Christ Jesus." They challenge us to find light even in our darkest valleys, to discover blessing even in our desert seasons.

When life's challenges loom before us like towering mountains, we often make the mistake of standing too close—like trying to comprehend a masterpiece with our noses pressed against the canvas. We need to step back, to climb higher, to see our lives from heaven's vantage point. Imagine yourself rising above your current circumstances, like an eagle soaring on thermal currents, until your trials below become part of a larger landscape of grace.

From this elevated perspective, today's struggles take their proper place in the vast panorama of your journey. See how the dark valleys of your past have led to sunlit peaks of triumph? Notice how previous storms, now weathered, have carved strength into your character like rivers shaping canyons? Each challenge you've overcome stands as a memorial stone, testifying to God's faithfulness. The One who parted yesterday's Red Sea still holds tomorrow's victories in His hands.

## Problems and Temptations: Wrestling with Giants and Shadows

There's an old saying that echoes through church halls: 'Don't tell God you have a big problem; tell your problem you have a big God.' Although this sentiment holds some truth, it fails to capture the profound depth of our connection with the Divine. Our Creator doesn't merely want our proclamations of His power—He longs for our honest outpouring of heart, our raw confessions of struggle, and our trembling admissions of fear. Like a father who gathers his child into his arms, God extends this tender invitation through Matthew 11:28: "Come to me, all you who are weary and burdened, and I will give you rest." These aren't just words on a page—they're a divine embrace, a sacred invitation to bring every burden, no matter how small, to the throne of Grace.

In the depths of His infinite wisdom, God already holds intimate knowledge of every shadow that darkens our path, every thorn that pierces our heart. Yet still He beckons us to come, to pour out our stories like precious oil at His feet. Why? Because in the sacred space of confession and communion, something profound happens—not a mere downloading of information, but a transformation of relationship. Like a master gardener tending to delicate shoots, God nurtures our trust through these vulnerable moments of sharing. Each time we open our heart's door to Him, the roots of our faith grow deeper, stronger, and more resilient. This is the beautiful paradox of prayer:

## THE BOY FROM BRAZIL

though He knows all, He longs to hear it from our lips, to cradle our concerns in His hands, and to transform our act of sharing into an altar of intimacy.

Through the corridors of church history echoes a familiar teaching, one that's brought both comfort and confusion: "God will not give us problems beyond our ability to bear." Like a well-worn coin, this phrase has passed through countless hands, often paired with the words of 1 Corinthians 10:13: "No temptation has overtaken you except what is common to mankind. And God is faithful; he will not let you be tempted beyond what you can bear. But when you are tempted, he will also provide a way out so that you can endure it."

These words shimmer with promise, like starlight piercing storm clouds. Yet to truly grasp their meaning, we must examine them with both heart and mind, understanding the subtle but crucial distinction between life's trials and temptation's snares.

Here we encounter a vital truth: this passage speaks specifically of temptation—that seductive serpent that winds through the garden of our lives, wearing countless disguises but always carrying the same poison. Unlike other trials that we're called to face with courage, temptation demands a different response: strategic retreat. This wisdom echoes through the centuries in the story of Joseph, whose decisive flight from temptation still teaches us today. His tale unfolds in Genesis 39:6-12, a dramatic scene that plays out like sacred theater:

*"Now Joseph was well-built and handsome, and after a while, his master's wife noticed Joseph and said, 'Come to bed with me!' But he refused. "With me in charge," he told her, "my master does not concern himself with anything in the house; everything he owns he has entrusted to my care. No one is greater in this house than I am. My master has withheld nothing from me except you because you are his wife. How then could I do such a wicked thing and sin against God?" And though she*

*spoke to Joseph day after day, he refused to go to bed with her or even be with her. One day he went into the house to attend to his duties, and none of the household servants was inside. She caught him by his cloak and said, "Come to bed with me!" But he left his cloak in her hand and ran out of the house."*

In this ancient drama, Joseph's flight wasn't mere cowardice—it was holy wisdom incarnate. He understood the perilous arithmetic of temptation: every moment spent in its presence amplifies its power. Potiphar's wife was more than just a mere tempter; she embodied an alluring combination of power, beauty, and enduring opportunity. Like a flame that grows hotter the longer you stand near it, her allure was designed to wear down even the strongest resolve. The very fact that she possessed such compelling beauty underscores the nature of true temptation—it always comes wrapped in packages that appeal to our deepest desires.

Our flight from temptation acknowledges a profound truth about human nature: we run precisely because standing still ensures our eventual surrender. Like a master strategist, temptation studies our unique vulnerabilities, crafting custom-made snares for each soul. What proves an irresistible lure for one may hold no power over another—a feast might be a battleground of willpower for some, while others pass by untroubled. Digital temptations can deafen some, while leaving others unmoved. This is why wisdom doesn't call us to test our strength against temptation's current, but rather to recognize our personal weak spots and chart our course far from those treacherous waters. In this battle, victory often wears the mask of apparent retreat.

The scripture's reminder that "no temptation has overtaken you except what is common to mankind" carries both comfort and challenge. It whispers that we're not alone in our struggles, while simultaneously calling us to the wisdom of self-knowledge. Like a seasoned

# THE BOY FROM BRAZIL 179

sailor who knows which waters harbor hidden reefs, we must become intimate students of our own hearts, mapping the territories where our resolve tends to weaken.

While wisdom encourages us to avoid temptation, it necessitates a distinct approach when confronted with real-life challenges. Here, we must maintain our ground, akin to ancient oaks enduring harsh weather conditions. Consider the iconic confrontation between David and Goliath—a moment when courage and faith collided with seemingly insurmountable odds. While seasoned warriors trembled in the shadow of the Philistine giant, a shepherd boy saw something different. While others perceived insurmountable challenges, David perceived a chance for divine intervention. Where veteran soldiers heard threatening roars, he heard empty boasts against his living God.

His declaration in 1 Samuel 17:45-47 rings through history like a battle cry of faith: "You come against me with sword and spear and javelin, but I come against you in the name of the Lord Almighty." These weren't mere words thrown into the wind—they were a testament to a profound understanding that true victory flows not from human might but divine power. David's bold proclamation that "the battle is the Lord's" wasn't bravado; it was a recognition that when we face our giants in God's name, we never face them alone.

Yet this truth carries a paradox, illuminated by the Apostle Paul's raw confession in 2 Corinthians 1:8-9. Here was a spiritual giant brought to his knees, admitting that his trials in Asia pressed him "far beyond our ability to endure." The pressure was so intense that death itself seemed to cast its shadow over him. But in this valley of despair, Paul discovered a revolutionary truth: Sometimes God allows challenges beyond our strength precisely so we'll stop relying on our own resources and lean fully into His limitless power. Like a master jeweler applying precise pressure to transform raw carbon into diamonds, God uses our moments of greatest weakness to forge our greatest strength—not our own, but His working through us.Paul acknowledged that the trials and problems they experienced were beyond their ability to endure, so they would rely on God fully in their lives. He continued in 1 Corinthians 12:6-9 when he said this...

Paul reveals his personal battle with divine purpose in one of scripture's most vulnerable confessions. His words in 1 Corinthians 12:6-9 reveal the profound paradox of spiritual strength:

*"Even if I should choose to boast, I would not be a fool, because I would be speaking the truth. But I refrain..."* Here stands a man who had every right to showcase his spiritual resume—heavenly visions, miraculous encounters, unprecedented revelations. Yet in the midst of these extraordinary experiences, God allowed a thorn to pierce his flesh, a persistent reminder of human frailty.

Three times Paul begged for deliverance, his prayers rising like incense toward heaven. But instead of removal, he received revelation: *"My grace is sufficient for you, for my power is made perfect in weakness."* This divine response transformed Paul's understanding of strength itself. Like a master artist who uses negative space to highlight beauty, God used Paul's weakness to showcase His power.

*"Therefore,"* Paul declares with hard-won wisdom, *"I will boast all the more gladly about my weaknesses so that Christ's power may rest on me."* This wasn't mere resignation to suffering—it was a revolutionary embrace of divine paradox. Through this lens, Paul's extraordinary ministry takes on new meaning. The man who penned nearly a third of the New Testament, who planted churches across the ancient world, who shaped Christian theology for millennia to come, did so not despite his weakness, but because of it. His thorn became a channel for grace; his limitations became showcases for divine power.

# THE BOY FROM BRAZIL

This great apostle's legacy stands not as a testament to human capability but as a monument to what happens when human weakness fully surrenders to divine strength. Every letter he penned, every church he founded, and every mile he traveled preaching the gospel stemmed from this profound understanding: our limitations often serve as God's launching pads.

## Worldviews: Navigating the Marketplace of Truth

In today's world, philosophies and beliefs crowd the intellectual marketplace like vendors in an ancient bazaar, each calling out their promises of enlightenment and fulfillment. These voices echo through social media feeds, whisper from bestseller lists, and broadcast from countless platforms, creating a cacophony of competing truths. Similar to sailors navigating through fog, we can easily become disoriented in this sea of ideologies.

But in this swirling mist of human wisdom, one lighthouse stands eternal—the unchanging Word of God. While the Bible may not serve as an encyclopedia for every conceivable question, it provides something far more vital: a divine compass for navigating life's complex moral and spiritual terrain. Like a master key that opens the essential doors of understanding, Scripture illuminates the path to victorious living.

Writing with the wisdom of years spent walking with Christ, the Apostle John issues a clear call that still resonates today: "Beloved, do not believe every spirit, but test the spirits to see whether they are from God, for many false prophets have gone out into the world" (1 John 4:4). These words ring with particular urgency in our age of instant information and viral ideologies.

Consider the methods of those who guard against counterfeit currency: Federal agents don't spend their days examining fake bills. Instead, they immerse themselves in studying genuine currency, meticulously examining every ridge and memorizing every security feature, until they become accustomed to the authentic. When a counterfeit appears, its falseness rings out like a discordant note in a symphony.

This same principle guides our spiritual discernment. Rather than attempting to master every philosophical system or deconstruct every false teaching, we're called to steep ourselves in truth. By dwelling deeply in Scripture, allowing its wisdom to permeate our understanding like water into soil, we develop a spiritual sensitivity that naturally detects deviation from divine truth. The Bible becomes our touchstone, not just for spotting falsehood but for understanding the very nature of our human condition—including the ancient roots of our struggle with sin.

## The Fallen Nature of Man: Echo of Eden's Fracture

In the primordial garden, where paradise once breathed in perfect harmony with its Creator, a single choice shattered the mirror of divine fellowship. The words spoken to Adam still reverberate through the corridors of time, each syllable heavy with consequence:

"Because you listened to your wife and ate fruit from the tree about which I commanded you, 'You must not eat from it,' cursed is the ground because of you; through painful toil, you will eat food from it all the days of your life. It will produce thorns and thistles for you, and you will eat the plants of the field. By the sweat of your brow, you will eat your food until you return to the ground since from it, you were taken; for dust you are and to dust you will return" (Genesis 3:17-19).

# THE BOY FROM BRAZIL          183

These words signify the significant break—the instant when harmony fractured into discord, ease transformed into labor, and immortality surrendered to dust. Like ripples spreading from a stone cast into still waters, the consequences of that first disobedience continue to touch every shore of human experience. The fruit taken from the Tree of Knowledge of Good and Evil became the seed of all human suffering, its bitter taste lingering in every generation's mouth.

This ancestral wound, this primal tear in the fabric of creation, isn't merely a historical narrative—it's the diagnostic key that explains humanity's persistent struggle with divine intent. Sin entered our story not as a mere mistake but as a fundamental reimagining of human identity, a tragic declaration of independence from the Source of all good.

The power of this inherited brokenness reveals itself in humanity's persistent inability to bridge the chasm back to God through our own efforts. The Apostle Paul captures this universal struggle in his haunting confession in Romans 7:17: "As it is, it is no longer I who do it, but it is sin living in me." Here we encounter the great paradox of human nature—the twilight war between our highest aspirations and our deepest inclinations. "For I desire to do what is good, but I cannot carry it out. For what I do is not the good I want to do; no, the evil I do not want to do—this I keep on doing." These words paint the portrait of humanity's inner civil war, where victory seems forever out of reach through human strength alone.

Paul's struggle illuminates our own—this perpetual warfare between divine aspiration and human frailty. Like gravity's constant pull, our fallen nature exerts its influence on every choice, every intention. Without the guidance of divine grace, we inevitably gravitate towards darkness instead of light. Kay Arthur's insight, which pierces the core of sin's deceptive nature, powerfully expresses this truth:

*"Sin will take you farther than you ever expected to go; it will keep you longer than you ever intended to stay, and it will cost you more than you ever expected to pay."*

These words echo with the wisdom of countless shattered dreams and broken promises. Like a spider's web that appears delicate yet binds with surprising strength, sin entangles us in its sticky threads one small choice at a time. We find ourselves, like wanderers following shifting lights, led ever deeper into spiritual wilderness, far beyond our intended destination.

The evidence of sin's mastery over human nature reveals itself in our repeated surrender to temptations we sincerely wished to resist. Like prisoners rattling the bars of our cell, we feel the frustration of wanting freedom yet finding ourselves bound. This paradox drew from Paul one of Scripture's most poignant cries: "Oh, what a miserable person I am! Who will rescue me from this life that is dominated by sin and death?" His words capture the universal human experience—that moment when we realize our own strength is insufficient for the battle we face.

To understand sin merely as transgression against moral law is to grasp only its shadow. Sin runs deeper than mere violation of rules—it is a cosmic treason, a fundamental disruption of the harmony God intended for creation. Like a stone cast into a still pond, each sin sends ripples of discord through the fabric of existence itself. The Hebrew word for sin, "chata," literally means "to miss the mark"—not just falling short of some arbitrary standard, but failing to fulfill our created purpose, like an arrow straying from its intended target.

Christianity's heart resonates with the rhythm of redemption precisely because it recognizes the profound wound in human nature. Sin isn't merely breaking divine rules—it's breaking the divine heart. Each transgression represents not just an offense against the law but

## THE BOY FROM BRAZIL                    185

a personal betrayal of the Lawgiver, a turning away from the face of infinite love.

This truth finds its most poignant illustration in the story of King David—a man whose great sin cast long shadows across the pages of Scripture. In a moment of unchecked desire, this "man after God's own heart" orchestrated a tragedy of Shakespearean proportions: adultery with Bathsheba, the betrayal and murder of Uriah (one of his most loyal warriors), and the attempted cover-up of his crimes. Yet in the aftermath of these grievous sins, David's heart-rending confession in Psalm 51:4 reveals a profound understanding:

*"Against you, you only, have I sinned and done what is evil in your sight; so you are right in your verdict and justified when you judge."*

These words pierce to the heart of sin's true nature. Though David's actions had devastated multiple lives—Bathsheba, Uriah, their families, and ultimately his own kingdom—he recognized that the deepest wound was inflicted upon God Himself. By Mosaic Law, his crimes demanded death, yet in this moment of brutal self-honesty before God, David discovered something remarkable: the height of divine justice is matched by the depth of divine mercy.

From the ashes of David's repentance rises one of Scripture's most powerful testimonies to redemption. Though his sins were scarlet, they did not write the final chapter of his story. The God who could have condemned instead chose to restore, demonstrating that our darkest failures need not become our defining identity. As the final testimony of his life declares, "Now *when David had served God's purpose in his generation, he fell asleep"* (Acts 13:36). These simple words carry profound hope—even after catastrophic failure, David fulfilled his divine purpose.

The miracle of David's story echoes through millennia—despite the gravity of his transgressions, history remembers him not as the king who fell but as the man after God's own heart. This paradox illuminates the radical nature of divine grace. Like a master artist who incorporates flaws into an even more beautiful masterpiece, God wove David's failures into a tapestry of redemption that still inspires hope today.

This truth stands as an eternal beacon for all who feel trapped by their past mistakes or present struggles. Your story, like David's, is still being written. The pen hasn't dropped; the final chapter remains unfinished. Just as a symphony builds through movements of both discord and harmony to reach its triumphant conclusion, your life's purpose can still find its full expression in God's grand composition.

The invitation remains open—not just to receive forgiveness, but to experience complete restoration. Like branches grafted back into the vine, we can reconnect with our divine purpose. This isn't merely about second chances; it's about transformation so complete that our scars become testimonies of grace. Perfect performance is not the key, but perfect positioning: be with God, stay with God, allow His presence to become your home, and make His purpose your compass.

This restoration journey enables us to comprehend an additional aspect of sin's essence, which Scripture characterizes as "falling short" of God's expectations for humanity. This isn't merely about small missteps or accidental stumbles. Like an archer who deliberately aims away from their target, humanity's original sin represented a conscious choice to stray from divine alignment. When Adam and Eve reached for the forbidden fruit, they weren't merely making a mistake—they were actively choosing to redirect their aim from God's perfect will to their own desires. Their story serves as a mirror reflecting our own daily choices between divine alignment and self-directed wandering.

Perhaps no modern illustration better captures this concept of "missing the mark" than the heartbreaking story from the 2004

Olympic Games. Matt Emmons, an American marksman, stood poised on the threshold of glory in the three-position rifle event. Picture the scene: an athlete at the pinnacle of his sport, having mastered the demanding art of shooting from stomach, knees, and feet, with thousands of hours of training crystallized into this moment. Leading the competition, with gold virtually assured, Emmons took careful aim at what he thought was his target—only to discover he had been shooting at the wrong lane. Suddenly, years of preparation and a certain victory evaporated into an eighth-place finish.

This Olympic tragedy serves as a powerful metaphor for humanity's spiritual condition. Like Emmons, we might execute our lives with apparent precision—maintaining careful aim, applying disciplined effort, and demonstrating technical excellence—and yet still miss the true target completely. The tragedy isn't in lacking skill or effort; it's in aiming at the wrong goal altogether. Just as the most perfectly executed shot at the wrong target earns zero points, so too can a life lived with precision and purpose still miss its divine intention if aimed away from God's glory.

But this story carries even deeper spiritual resonance. In Olympic shooting, there is no partial credit for hitting the wrong target, no matter how accurately. Similarly, in our spiritual journey, we cannot create our own markers of success or redefine the target of God's perfect will. The divine standard isn't about approximation—it's about alignment with God's perfect purpose for our lives.

## The Gospel: The Divine Response to Human Tragedy

In the economy of sin, the ledger is clear and uncompromising. Romans 6:23 strikes like a judge's gavel: "For the wages of sin is death." This divine accounting carries no minimum threshold—a single sin earns death's wages in full. The sovereignty of this spiritual law towers over human history like an immutable mountain, its shadow falling across every life that has ever drawn breath.

This death manifests in two profound dimensions. First comes physical mortality—that inescapable return to dust pronounced in Genesis 3:19. Consider the poignant tragedy: Adam and Eve, created for eternal communion in Eden's garden, their bodies designed for immortality, now bearing death like a genetic mutation passed to every generation. The paradise that should have been their eternal home became a lost dream, its gates guarded by flaming swords.

But physical death merely foreshadows an even deeper catastrophe—spiritual death. This second death works like a slow-acting poison in the human soul, manifesting in symptoms we all recognize: the hollow ache of guilt that no achievement can fill, the gnawing emptiness that no pleasure can satisfy, and the cosmic loneliness that no relationship can fully bridge. Like a compass needle suddenly freed from magnetic north, our spirits spin in desperate search of meaning and connection.

Isaiah 59:2 captures this spiritual quarantine with haunting precision: "But your iniquities have separated you from your God; your sins have hidden his face from you so that he will not hear." This verse reveals sin's most devastating consequence—not just moral failure or guilty conscience, but cosmic exile from the very Source of life and love. Like a branch severed from its vine, humanity withers in its separation from divine life. And here lies the terrible culmination of this spiritual death: those who remain spiritually dead face an eternity of that separation in Hell—the final crystallization of their chosen alienation from God.

There's a dangerous misconception floating through modern spiritual discourse, captured in the notion that "the good news isn't that

# THE BOY FROM BRAZIL

good because the bad news isn't that bad." This casual dismissal of sin's gravity reveals our culture's spiritual anesthesia—a numbing of our moral nerves to eternal realities. Like patients who mistake a doctor's grave diagnosis for mere inconvenience, we risk fatal self-deception.

Jesus himself, the embodiment of divine love, spoke with stark clarity about these eternal consequences. His words in Mark 9:47-48 cut through all comfortable illusions: "And if your eye causes you to stumble, pluck it out. You should enter the kingdom of God with one eye than have two eyes and be thrown into hell, where the worms that eat them do not die, and the fire is not quenched." This isn't metaphorical hyperbole—it's divine warning wrapped in vivid imagery. The Master Physician speaks candidly about spiritual cancer.

The final verdict echoes with terrifying finality in Revelation 20:15: "And whosoever was not found written in the book of life was cast into the lake of fire." These words should strike our hearts like thunder, awakening us from spiritual slumber. Imagine a massive ledger of life, its pages containing the names of those chosen for eternal communion with God. The absence of one's name from this book isn't merely unfortunate—it's catastrophic. Like being erased from existence itself, yet remaining conscious to experience that erasure eternally.

This sobering reality forces us to confront the most urgent question any human can face: How can we ensure our names are inscribed in this book of life? Paul's words to the Philippians, "Yes, I ask you also, true companion, to help these women, who have labored side by side with me in the gospel along with Clement and the rest of my fellow workers, whose names are in the book of life," illuminate the possibility of such an inscription like the first light of dawn (Philippians 4:3). These words reveal both the possibility and the preciousness of having one's name recorded in heaven's eternal registry.

To have one's name written in the book of life isn't merely about avoiding hell—it's about gaining heaven itself. It means securing a place in the divine presence, where joy flows like rivers and love burns like holy fire. It means joining that great company of the redeemed who stand before the throne of God, their faces reflecting the light of His glory.

Thank God that Romans 6:23 did not just end in that statement, "For the wages of sin is death," but continues, saying this, "but the gift of God is eternal life in Christ Jesus our Lord."

But here the divine narrative takes an unexpected turn—where justice meets mercy in history's most dramatic moment. The infinite chasm carved by sin between humanity and God required a bridge of equally infinite span. God's own Son, not timber and stone, built that bridge. Like a master composer transforming dissonance into harmony, God crafted salvation from the very materials of our condemnation.

Hebrews 9:26-28 captures this cosmic transaction with breathtaking clarity: "But now he has appeared once for all at the end of the ages to get away with sin by the sacrifice of himself. Just as man is destined to die once and, after that, to face judgment, so Christ was sacrificed once to take away the sins of many people; and he will appear a second time, not to bear sin, but to bring salvation to those who are waiting for him." Here we see the divine mathematics of redemption—one perfect life paying the infinite debt of countless broken ones.

This Jesus, this cornerstone of salvation, stands as the great divide in human history. As Acts 4:11-12 declares with unwavering certainty: "This Jesus is 'the stone you builders rejected, which has become the cornerstone.' Salvation exists in no one else, for there is no other name under heaven given to men by which we must be saved." Like a master key that fits every lock of human bondage, Christ's sacrifice opens the

# THE BOY FROM BRAZIL

single door to eternal life. All other paths, no matter how noble or sincere, lead only to dead ends in the maze of human striving.

In Him, the mathematics of divine justice finds its perfect solution—where the infinite cost of sin meets the infinite worth of the Son of God. Like a mighty river cutting through an impassable mountain, His sacrifice carved the only pathway back to God's presence.

The path to salvation emerges when we finally exhaust our own spiritual resources—when, like shipwrecked sailors abandoning their sinking vessel, we cease clinging to the wreckage of self-reliance and reach for the lifeline of divine grace. This sacred transaction occurs at the intersection of divine provision and human response, where our desperate need meets God's infinite supply.

Romans 10:9-10 crystallizes this transformative moment: "You will be saved if you confess with your mouth that Jesus is Lord and believe in your heart that God raised him from the dead." For it is with your heart that you believe and are justified, and it is with your mouth that you confess and are saved." Like a key fitting perfectly into a lock, this dual action of heart and mouth opens the door to eternal life.

Standing at this decision-making threshold, positioned between your past and God's future, this moment bears the weight of eternity. The words that follow aren't merely a formula or religious ritual—they're the language of surrender, the vocabulary of new birth. Let them rise from the depths of your being as your own authentic cry to God:

## A Prayer of New Beginning

"Eternal Father,

I stand before You now, finally seeing the infinite distance my sins have carved between us. Like scales falling from my eyes, I recognize the depth of my need and the height of Your holiness. I acknowledge that every step I've taken away from You has only led me deeper into darkness.

Thank you for sending Jesus—your perfect Son—to bridge this impossible chasm. I believe with all my heart that He died in my place, bearing the full weight of my sins on Calvary's cross. I believe that death could not hold Him, that He rose victorious from the grave, and that He lives today offering new life to all who turn to Him.

I turn now from my self-directed path, from every sin that has entangled me, from every false refuge I've trusted. I open my life fully to Your leadership, surrendering every corner of my being to Your authority. Cleanse me, recreate me, and set my feet on Your path.

From this day forward, I choose to follow You, to love what You love, to build my life on the foundation of Your truth. Let Your Spirit fill me, Your love transform me, and Your purpose guide me.

In Jesus' name, Amen."

If you've prayed these words with a sincere heart, heaven itself rejoices. Like a new star blazing to life in the cosmic darkness, your name now shines in the eternal registry of the redeemed. This moment marks not an ending but a beginning—the first breath of your new existence in Christ.

But just as a newborn needs nurture and guidance, your spiritual birth requires support and community. Seek out a vibrant church where God's Word stands as the cornerstone of teaching, where

# THE BOY FROM BRAZIL 193

Christ's love flows through genuine relationships, where fellow believers can walk alongside you in this grand adventure of faith. Like a young eagle learning to soar, you'll need both instruction and inspiration from those who have already learned to ride the winds of grace.

## The Time to Emerge: Your Spiritual Metamorphosis

Nature itself testifies to the reality of transformation through the miracle of metamorphosis. Just as a caterpillar must pass through the darkness of its chrysalis before emerging as a butterfly, many of us have dwelt in spiritual darkness, wrapped in cocoons of doubt, fear, or past regrets. But now, through Christ, the time of emergence has come.

This transformation isn't merely about leaving behind the old—it's about embracing the glorious identity for which you were created. Like a butterfly spreading its newly formed wings, you're called to display the beauty of God's craftsmanship in your life. As naturally as these transformed creatures seek nectar from flowers, may your spirit be drawn to the sweet presence of God, drinking deeply from the wells of divine wisdom and righteousness.

Feel the holy freedom that comes with this rebirth. Like a bird released from its cage, your spirit can now soar in the updrafts of divine purpose. The past, with all its failures and regrets, no longer defines you. What matters now is not the person you were, but the one you're becoming in Christ—His masterpiece, His beloved, His testimony to the world of grace's transforming power.

This is your moment of emergence. Step into the light. Spread your wings. Soar.

As we reach the close of this shared journey, my heart brims with gratitude for your willingness to walk these pages with me. Every story shared, every truth explored, every moment of vulnerability has been offered with a single hope: that somewhere in these words, you might encounter the living God who transformed my own life from ashes to beauty.

If even one soul finds their way home to the Father through this humble offering of words and experiences, then every sentence will have served its sacred purpose. Like a lighthouse keeper who tends the flame through countless nights, knowing that even one ship guided safely to harbor justifies all effort, I release these words into the world with prayer and expectation.

May your own story, wherever it leads from here, be illuminated by the unfailing light of divine love. For in the end, every human narrative finds its true meaning only when it becomes part of God's greater story of redemption.

# About the Author

Marcelo Sousa is an accomplished educator, writer, and certified Christian coach with nearly two decades of experience in education. Currently pursuing his doctorate in Educational Leadership at Liberty University, he holds a master's degree in TESOL/Bilingual Education and a sixth-year degree in Educational Leadership from Southern Connecticut State University, building upon his foundation in History and Elementary Education from Kean University.

A Brazilian-born American educator, Mr. Sousa has established himself as an authority in multilingual education and teacher development. His diverse background includes performing arts experience in New York City's theater scene, bringing a unique creative perspective to his educational approach. As a Certified Christian Coach from The Center for Christian Coaching (CCC), he integrates spiritual guidance with educational leadership.

An internationally recognized speaker, Mr. Sousa regularly conducts workshops and presentations worldwide, sharing his expertise in multilingual education and educational leadership. His commitment to fostering inclusive learning environments and empowering educators has made him a sought-after voice in the field.

When not writing or teaching, he continues to inspire audiences through his public speaking engagements across the globe. **Info@theboyfrombrazil.org** Website: **theboyfrombrazil.org** Professional Social Media: Tiktok: **@theboyfrombrazil** / Instagram: **the_boy_from_brazil**

Made in the USA
Middletown, DE
01 May 2025

74989888R00113